NAVIGATING THE CLOUDS

Jody Gold

WESTBOW
PRESS®
A DIVISION OF THOMAS NELSON
& ZONDERVAN

WestBow Press books may be ordered through booksellers or by contacting:

WestBow Press
A Division of Thomas Nelson & Zondervan
1663 Liberty Drive
Bloomington, IN 47403
www.westbowpress.com
1 (866) 928-1240

ISBN: 978-1-9736-3317-4 (sc)
ISBN: 978-1-9736-3316-7 (hc)
ISBN: 978-1-9736-3318-1 (e)

Library of Congress Control Number: 2018907812

Print information available on the last page.

WestBow Press rev. date: 8/30/2018

This book is dedicated to all those far and near who, without your love, support, and many prayers, this book would not have become a reality. A special heartfelt hug to Julia and Vikki for your editing skills and endless encouragement. To my dear friend April, thank you for always giving me just the advice I needed, and thanks for your friendship, which I cherish. To Ed, you are a wise man, and I appreciate your knowledge and truth, always. To my medical team, yes, it's your job, but we are all human, and every person you treat feels the warmth and kindness of your touch. Overwhelming love and respect to you all. To my community of friends, you are my family; you are my village. To my children, the depth of my love for you will never end. You are the most important people in my life. To my husband, I love you more.

CONTENTS

This book is about the individual and collective tenacity and strength of the human spirit. At its core is the power of love, given and received, to transform and to provide hope and encouragement during an unexpected life-changing journey. This book is not just about cancer, nor is it only for those facing cancer.

Having been alongside the author on her journey, I have seen firsthand the undeniable power of focusing outward. I have been forever changed by the experience; Jody's choice to look at the small positives along the way collectively resulted in unstoppable optimism and gratitude for even the tiniest blessings.

Navigating the Clouds will inspire you, challenge you, and most importantly, give you hope in your own life. It will also help you realize that even the smallest acts of kindness can have a lifetime of impact.

Victoria Miller

CHAPTER 1

Introduction

As I look around my living room on this sunny late morning weekday, I realize that God's plan for my book began some time ago. The types of books on my shelves tell a story that I had not seen or realized was there: titles of self-help, finding joy in every day, planning your day God's way, love languages, and many more. I believe that I have been searching for my purpose.

How my journey began: One day, I found a lump the size of a quarter in my left breast. I emailed my general practitioner to advise her and asked if I should come in for a visit. She rather urgently scheduled an appointment for the next day. I found no reason for worry on my end, since no one in my family has ever had breast cancer. The next day, she examined me and gave me some numbers to call and set up a follow-up appointment.

Before I left, she stood eye to eye with me and said, "Make the call as soon as you get in your car."

I did think this was strange but agreed. What transpired afterwards set the ball rolling for me and caused me to have a bit of concern. The institution I was being referred to could not see me for three weeks because they needed my mammograms. In previous years, I recalled that I had them done in a mobile unit outside of my husband's work. What should have only taken a few minutes took upwards of forty-five minutes while I was still in the car. My saving grace was a woman on the other end of the line at Swedish Medical Center, who informed me that they had all my films. At that point, I explained that an appointment could not be set up for three weeks.

She said, "Come here; we will see you tomorrow morning."

After I hung up the phone, I realized that this may be more serious than I had anticipated. The next day, with Glenn in tow, we went to the hospital, and I met with an ultrasound nurse, who immediately took me back for the test. There were not a lot of words spoken during this exam. At the time, I did not have any concern. Back in the lobby, another nurse approached me and asked if I could stay for a needle biopsy. Right now? Yes, of course.

As we waited in complete silence, I believed in my mind that there was no need to worry until the situation lent itself to such. I honestly don't know what Glenn was thinking at the time. We were ushered into another room with a staff of medical personnel and a team of gentle, caring folks, who explained every procedure they were going to perform on me. This was all new to me, so I did not have any expectations. From what I remember, they did two needle biopsies and sent me on my way. We were told that it would be a week or so before the results were available. I had no idea what results would come of this test. Glenn left on a business trip out of the country, as planned, and we never gave it another thought. Well, I didn't. In the weeks to come, the lives of me and my family would be forever changed.

A week later, on Friday, May 29, 2011, a doctor called me after five o'clock; she asked if I was driving. I thought that was strange. She asked me to sit down. Before I could even process what was going on, the word *cancer* was all I heard. What? How can that be? I was numb and sat for a while, just absorbing what I was told. At that point, I did not cry or have any thoughts of dying.

People survive cancer all the time, I thought. I remember keeping this information to myself for a couple of days and not wanting to worry anyone. I tried to avoid talking to Glenn before he returned home. I knew I could only give him this news face to face. He knew something was not right and continued to ask a lot of questions. I held it together long enough to have him at my side, so we would support each other during this time of uncertainty. I guess I never fully believed that this could happen unless there was a family history of breast cancer. I had a lot of questions.

Upon reflection, at the time of my diagnosis, there were things that happened that were out of character for me. I now believe one of the first things that I did was something the Lord had planned. At the time, I didn't even realize that going door to door on our small suburban cul-de-sac to tell every neighbor that I had breast cancer was out of the ordinary. Why would I do this? The events that ensued were beyond what I could have ever imagined. As days passed and the word spread throughout our small community, I could not emotionally prepare myself for the enormous number of folks who appeared out of the woodwork to come to my and my family's aid. People wanted to help in any way they could. Day after day, friends and acquaintances came by and dropped off food, cards, gifts, and other offers of such magnitude that I could not comprehend. Many folks came in with hugs and others with arms stretched out for prayer. I spent time in the doorway with many who just wanted to pray for me without coming inside. I had reached out in a way that had touched so many lives.

As people came and left, every day, I was overcome with

emotion. Why did so many people support us, love us, and take time out of their busy lives to care for us? The Holy Spirit was hard at work in me. I didn't feel like myself and began to see things in a way I had never seen before. I thought I hadn't deserved their care or even earned their love, for that matter. After every visit, I began to have the faith that would light my way. This was something I had not experienced before.

At the time, my kids were in seventh, ninth, and eleventh grades. My life was full. I was working part-time for the school district and had just volunteered to be on the board of one of the community groups at school. One of the hardest things that I had to do was tell people in person about what was about to happen in my life. I was not sure that I could continue to work or even volunteer. I'd never had cancer before. I had not been around anyone who had gone through it. I had no idea what to expect. What I did know is that each person I told was devastated and upset. This continued to weigh heavily on my heart. I needed to find another way to reach out. I could not take the tears and hugs every time. I just couldn't. It hurt too much.

By this time, everyone at Glenn's office got word, and he was experiencing some of the same feelings. I could see this was going to be difficult to keep up. After one of my appointments, I decided to write an email update about where I was in my journey and include as much detail as possible. So much of it I could not remember, let alone relate to those who inquired. I decided to share these updates with you as they reflect my thoughts, feelings, and experiences during my journey. It is my hope that they will give you inspiration, hope, and wisdom as you navigate your own journey.

This would be my first email, sent fifteen days later:

Sent: Sun 6/12/11 2:32 p.m.

Hi there: I regret that I'm not personally calling you. It is with a heavy heart that I am sending this. I found out last week that I have breast cancer. I am in the middle of trying to deal with many things and am an emotional mess. I'm writing to find out if you would be willing to provide a meal for my family in the next two weeks? I have a friend who is going to be handling the coordination of days and be in touch with you if you decide you can help. Please do not feel obligated. Fortunately, there has been a huge amount of support for which I am deeply grateful. I will just be providing a list. I will find out this Friday, June 17, 2011, when my surgery will take place. It will be soon. I will have a three-week recovery after that and a team of loving people who are seeing to my care and my families' care.

Please do not hesitate to contact me by email this week with questions or by phone. I don't have a lot of answers at this point. I hope you will understand. With gratitude, Jody

This was a difficult note to write, but the responses were incredible. Everyone wanted information and details. I believe for many people in our community, it was their first time going through cancer treatment with a friend.

CHAPTER 2

Investigation

Here is my next email, seven days later.

June 19, 2011, 12:18 a.m.

Here is the latest. I'm sorry not to call. I was at Swedish every day last week. At this time, surgery has been put on hold. I will be at Swedish next week on Monday, Tuesday, and Wednesday. After several tests, it was determined that a spot (not determined cancer at this time) was found in my chest wall. Since this is an inoperable area, my oncologist has told us that I have stage 4 limited. This means that since there may be a chance it's in the chest, we have to proceed with chemotherapy first.

I have a procedure on Tuesday that is called something like a bronchoscopy (an ultrasound-directed biopsy). They put me to sleep and do a biopsy of the spot in question. There is a chance that it is not cancer. I have a highly active and fast-spreading cancer.

On Wednesday, they will put me to sleep again to insert a port in my chest to receive chemotherapy. I will have a blood test to determine my white blood count and a MUGA test to determine the health of my heart since chemo can make the lining of the heart thin.

After all of this, I believe chemo starts on the week of the twenty-seventh. It will be very aggressive in my case. So six months of chemotherapy, once a week every other week. My mother-in-love arrived today. The thought is that after my first treatment, I will be down for a week and be better by the second, and this will continue in the same order. Weak and tired and hopefully not sick.

Really not looking forward to this but I will do whatever is needed. I have a wonderful team of doctors. It's going to be a long, emotional road, and it's taking a toll already. My family and I will need the love and support of all the wonderful people in our lives! I will need things to keep my mind off my treatments. The doctor says to exercise, including walking, when I'm ready, and hopefully cooking in my new kitchen after next week.

Had a very fun day today. I'm not letting cancer keep my every thought.

Love, Jody

Five days later, I had some good news to report.

June 24, 12:35 a.m.

Wanted to share with you some good news.

Just found out on the genetic test results that I am negative for the markers that indicate a genetic mutation that would carry on to my children and have other effects. This is such a relief.

On a bigger and much scarier scale, last week the oncologist indicated that during my PET CT scan, it was discovered that three of my lymph nodes lit up in my chest. To verify them as infected or not, I had a bronchoscopy (an ultrasound-directed biopsy through my throat). This was the reason for going straight to chemotherapy. The chest area around the lungs and heart is not an area that can be operated on. My doctor indicated that I was a stage 4 limited based on this chest area. As you can imagine, we were more than scared by this. Today, the preliminary results came back negative, which means that all three nodes that were biopsied were not infected. This was cause for celebration and brought a flood of emotion by all.

We appreciate all your love and prayers and feel so grateful to have so many wonderful friends with big hearts in our lives.

With love, Jody

CHAPTER 3

First Round

My general practitioner (GP), whom I originally saw when I discovered the lump, was getting all the medical information from the Swedish system. She was not up-to-date on my care. She has been my GP for seventeen years now, and I have a great relationship with her. She did not know how I was coping with these events. Below is a special update directed to her.

June 29, 9:19 p.m.

> Not sure what's up but I imagine all the test results are en route to you. Maybe it's just taking a little longer considering the volume. Bronchoscopy went very well and results were negative on all three nodes (thank goodness). What a relief!

> The genetic testing also came back negative for both markers (more good news). Had port put in last Wednesday. Sore but went well too.

> Today I had my first chemotherapy session. The first twenty minutes is for antinausea medication. Then on with all of the other drugs with names I cannot remember, but Glenn has the information. He is busy

at work putting all my medications in order on my calendar so I know what to take and when.

Oh, the doctor mentioned that walking every day will keep me healthy and in good spirits. So I went for a thirty-minute walk when we got home with a bit of a rest in between. I also set up time with friends to come walk with me. I'm tired right now. Hope this all makes sense.

I'm doing okay but lost it in the oncologist's office. I burst into tears just talking about shaving my head! I have a wig on order and a cap I already bought for sleeping. You know, some times are better than others. We talked through it, and the nurse was kind and caring and had some suggestions on how to make it a family event. She also suggested that I should bring each of the kids separately to a chemo treatment. This would give them a better understanding of what happens and will most likely ease their fears of whatever they have been coming up with on their own. It's not been easy with them. I imagine once we shave my head, things will come to the surface, and we can go from there. I have my mother-in-love here. She's wonderful.

A friend of mine is putting my kitchen back together. We started a kitchen remodel just before we found out about my breast cancer. It's coming together but just slower than we all would have liked. I had dinner at a friend's house and have scheduled dinners coming every other night all month.

I have a ton of wonderful people all coming together to support all of us. Glenn's mom is going on walks daily with all my friends who offered to walk with her. This is good for all of them. I'm overwhelmed with emotion by the generosity and kindness we have been shown. Feel free to share this information with Ed, if you'd like.

Glenn is going to be setting up something online with updates. He has just been so busy with me, the kitchen remodel, refinance, and many duties that I would normally handle. His office has been so kind to him and us. I'm sure he is overwhelmed as well. I'm going to send him for a deep-tissue massage soon, like it or not! Probably more than you expected.

Take care, Jody

An uplifting day shared.

July 2, 11:55 p.m.

Hi, everyone! It's been a wonderful day around here. Except someone decided to blow our mailbox to kingdom come last night around 2:30 a.m. Not kidding. The front landed on our neighbors' roof across the street while the back landed in our backyard, and the middle— well, it's unrecognizable! Oh well. I guess we needed a new one. Headed for Home Depot. Fortunately we had other items to get for our new kitchen, in addition to a new mailbox. That was my walk for the day! Very successful, I might say.

I then sat in the sun, enjoyed the afternoon at home, and got some unpacking done in the kitchen (with Grandma's help). Put in new lights and mailbox, watered some plants, and listened to some music. Anyway, you get the idea. You must all have been out enjoying it as well. Not a single word on email. Fabulous! It's late and I'm feeling great and wanted to share ...

Love to you all, Jody

When one of Glenn's coworkers heard what we were going through, she wanted to do something. I thought that it was more important to take care of the person taking care of me. Everything else could wait. This is my response to her inquiry.

July 9, 12:31 a.m.

Hi, T: [Glenn] sent me a copy of your email, and I wanted to personally contact you. Glenn has lots of ideas on what can be done around here (like most men). He is so far in over his head that he's not sure if he's coming or going at this point. I'm very worried about him and his well-being. It's enough to be the breadwinner, husband, and father, but being the caregiver as well has already taken its toll, and we are in for a long haul of it.

Please let me know what you think of this: I propose a day of caring for him at the health club. He could get a deep-tissue massage and maybe some soaking service of relaxation and lunch. This should take a great deal of time, and I can arrange it with my chemo schedule so that he doesn't have to worry about me. I'm afraid he's going to drop soon, and what will I do without him? I certainly need him to be strong, healthy, and somewhat rested, and I know that all these challenges are wearing him down.

I'm overwhelmed with the amount of love and support from an entire community of people I barely know. I know if the tables were turned he would want me to be well taken care of too. So I'm counting on you and the people on his team to help him get the love and care he needs to stay strong for his family and coworkers. I think everything else just doesn't matter right now.

My heart goes out to you, and know that my family and I are deeply grateful for your love and caring expressed in the emails sent to Glenn. It is truly comforting having so many friends with their arms open, willing and ready to provide whatever is needed. Please let me know what you need from me. Take care. Warmly, Jody

This update was sent twelve days later. Very soon after treatment began, the emotional part of me came rising to the surface. I felt like things were progressing much faster than I was prepared for.

Sent: Thu 7/14/11 3:18 p.m.

Thank all of you for your prayers. I had my second chemotherapy yesterday. It was a long day and I didn't feel so good. Came home and went to bed. Feeling better today. Just tired (which is part of it). Had to shave my head the day before chemo. This was, as you can imagine, very upsetting for me, and I didn't know how I was going to get through it. But I washed my hair Tuesday, and it was coming out, so I panicked and told Glenn we need to shave it tonight. Got Grandma and best friend for support, had a couple of glasses of wine, and went for it. I cried the whole time. It was awful! Glenn did the shaving while we all held on tight and cried. I cried most of the night. But the next morning, I could at least look in the mirror. Made it through that, thank goodness. I have some wigs that are cute and a hat for home. It was the weirdest feeling having no hair! I now look like a cancer patient which I haven't come to terms with yet.

I had some positive news from the oncologist at my follow-up appointment yesterday before chemotherapy. She checked my lymph nodes and lump. She could not feel the lymph nodes at all, and the lump was soft and significantly smaller for only having one treatment. We were all elated at this news! We wanted them to shrink asap so I could move on to the next step of removing them.

The power of prayer has been working in my life, and I appreciate all the support and love. It's difficult enough going through it but having loving people behind you just makes you feel so much better. Oh, before each chemotherapy treatment I must give blood. So when I got to the oncologist's office, I warned her that my blood alcohol level could be off the charts from last nights' event! We all laughed. It was funny. Thanks for all you do. I wanted to keep you updated on what's up with me. Love to you all, Jody

The constant contact with people outside my family was so incredibly important during my chemotherapy days. After leaving the hospital and nurses who were so supportive and positive, coming home can be very isolating.

In between treatments, we left town for a couple of days for a change of scenery and some quiet time to celebrate our anniversary.

Sent: Fri 7/22/11 12:19 p.m.

Where to begin? So much takes place in such a brief period of time. Treatment #2 was long and exhausting and did not come without some port pain, but I managed to make it through. I think that it doesn't matter how long or familiar the treatment is, it never becomes comfortable! It has taken longer to recover this time. Almost seven days! Looking back on the past four days, I've managed to digest and process many things that I would like to share:

Love is blind, and it does not see the bald. Glenn and I spent two days celebrating our twenty-first wedding anniversary at Salish Lodge, a nearby getaway. Glenn's mom treated us, and his coworkers set up a spa treatment for him. This time was not only precious but uplifting and rejuvenating. It is amazing how much stress our bodies can take without breaking down. While he destressed, I took in every moment of beauty and reflected on this journey. Everything could not have been more perfect. The falls were spectacular, and we took some photos. While looking at the photos, I realized that having hair did not make me who I am. As I often tell my kids, it's who you are on the inside that matters. This felt good because I think I am finally at peace with this bald head and don't see it as such an eyesore!

I was self-conscious about soaking in water with other guests and feared their uncomfortableness would jeopardize their stay. I was surprised, comforted, and relieved by their acceptance. While in the soaking pool with eyes closed, I realized that I was on my knees and looking up at the archway, reflecting on the quietness and warmth surrounding me. I felt God's presence and became emotional. I felt that He was showing me, together with all of you who surround me with your warmth and love, that I was going to be okay.

What an incredible feeling! I really felt as though I had everything: a husband, a family, a God, and friends who shower me with so much love. I can tell you what the emotional well-up was: a river of gratitude and gratefulness. I am energized and feel stronger.

Had my follow-up appointment on Wednesday. Wasn't feeling back to whatever normal is now and was fine until we got to the turn off on I-5. I realized that once again I was overcome with emotion. Just not wanting to go but knew I had to. Had blood taken, and results were the same as last time, but doctor indicated that I must not be around anyone who is, or is going to be, ill or I would end up in the hospital because of a low white blood count. Try relating this to teenage boys. :) I think that I was worried about what else was to come.

So through my tears, I asked, "What else is going to happen to me?" More hair loss, more sickness, more tiredness? I just want to prepare myself and my family for what's to come.

The nurse smiled and sat close and held my hand and said, "You're doing really well."

I said, "Eyebrows? Please, this is all the hair I have left."

She said possible eyelashes, hopefully not eyebrows. She reassured me that I would get a free Rustasis prescription, and my eyelashes would grow back.

All I could think of was, *Why, God? What else do I have to sacrifice to save my life?* I know, it's only hair. Okay, advantage and bright side to no hair is smoother, tanner legs that will stay tan longer because of no shaving; yahoo, I'll take it.

Onward. Yesterday a large envelope came from our insurance company, so I opened it to see that since June 2, my medical bills are nearly $70,000! As I flipped through page after page of all the tests and surgeries and injections, etc., I was completely overwhelmed by what I had been through so far in under sixty days of treatment. Again, the tears came and once again I realized that I'm so incredibly fortunate that my husband has a good job and that we have such incredible insurance. As I flipped through the bill, I noticed the amount we pay is zero. Once again thanking God! Glenn tells me all this emotion is good for me and is healing. I hope through this sharing that you will not feel my pain but know that we are sharing my journey of hope and strength together and that you are all my village, and I need you so. With love, Jody

Something I did not realize: I was still the same person everyone knew on the inside. Not looking like yourself can make you question how others think of you. All that people see is your appearance. It's sad feeling like you have no sense of identity. It's like looking into a mirror only to realize, Oh yeah, that's what everyone else sees. I remember running into a dear friend at the grocery store. We sat in my car to visit and catch up. I smiled through my tears, letting her know that I was all right. We hugged like we had always before. I could tell as we talked that she had a tough time looking at me, as I looked quite different. As I write this, I am reminded of a close friend who came to visit. She wanted to see me without my wig. As I removed it, she cried. We cried. It was real.

After going through this process, I realized that the loss of facial features as the result of chemotherapy treatment and a full head of hair do not seem like big sacrifices in order to save my life. They most certainly did so at the time. Perspective.

Sent: Thu 8/04/11 6:23 p.m.

Before I start on myself, I want you all to know how much you mean to me. Your kind words, cards, caring, and love keep me going and positive when at times it becomes too much. It's a week and a half after my last treatment, and I'm just coming around the corner to feeling ok. This remains my biggest challenge so far. After being treated last Wednesday, expecting to be feeling ok, it was quite the opposite. The cumulative effect of chemotherapy has taken its toll. I had my follow-up on Wednesday, yesterday, with a dear friend by my side.

The nurse, Betsy, said her pleasantries and smiled and said, "You still have your eyebrows." I smiled and said yes, hoping to keep them indefinitely and realizing that I may not have them much longer. I know this seems simple and silly, but the more things, like hair, eyebrows, eyelashes, you don't have, the more you look like you're sick or you're a cancer patient. I guess that I don't want people to think of me this way. It feels hurtful, and people look at you with sorrow and sadness. Which, as a cancer patient, you really don't want. You just want people to see you the way they always have (as yourself).

This feels like an incredible journey to undertake, which brings me to the book (one of many) that I have been reading: A *Daily Journal of Hope*, published by Family Christian Bookstores. As I read this book, I continue to look for meaning and growth on my journey to inspire me to be a better person for my family and others. The chapter on "The Wisdom of Obedience" spoke volumes to me! "God uses ordinary people who are obedient to Him to do extraordinary things." I'm not sure where it is all going, but I am hopeful and looking for my path, and I know that each of you are involved in some way, too.

I'm currently working on "The Art of Forgiveness," another chapter in the same book, thinking I have to do some forgiving of others but realizing that I may need to work on myself as well. Not sure if this makes any sense, but in searching for answers, I've come to realize that in my experience this week, I have not been persistent in helping those who may not be able or willing to ask for help. As I look inward, there are so many people in my life that have experienced heartache and loss that I've known about and not been persistent in seeing if they need help emotionally, spiritually, or physically. This makes me feel incredibly sad that I did not do more. There are so many people who needed love, conversation, and caring at a challenging time in their life, and I did not come forward. Feeling intrusive or fear of being rejected or just not knowing what to do. I'm not sure. I've realized that people are good and that we all need the same basic caring and love. I experienced this today when a neighbor was called by Glenn to check on me. I really did not want to be seen and was feeling like a mess. The simplest thing she did was come in and let me know it was okay to feel crummy and cry and that she would just sit with me and talk or just be here. Whew, it seems so simple!

Why is it so hard to ask for help? I don't really want people to know I'm feeling terrible. I realized today that I need to not only forgive myself for not doing more to comfort those I know who need it but reach out no matter what the circumstance is because I know how deeply I appreciate the love and concern that we all have for others, whether we know them completely or not. I'm not going to let that fear stand in the way of showing that I really do care and would do anything to help. There is an amazing feeling that comes from giving and receiving.

I don't believe bad things happen to good people, only that God gives us challenges to make us stronger.

I hope this note finds you happy and well and full of strength for whatever challenge lies ahead. With love, Jody

Sent: Tue 8/16/11 11:26 a.m.

I want to let you all know that today is a good day! I have finally finished my fourth chemotherapy treatment, which included mountains of drugs. But it's over now! And I couldn't be more thankful. My kids and husband probably are, too. I also want to let you know how so many of you have kept me going from day to day, from hour to hour. The dinners, cards, letters, balloons, notes of encouragement, books of faith and hope, your love and kindness, chocolates, cookies, bath salts, text messages daily, phone calls, flowers, fruits and vegetables from your gardens. Not to mention all the rides for my kids. I'm overcome with emotion and the amount of love that I feel from all of you. You genuinely warm my heart to tears.

My focus this week is on courageous perseverance in the face of difficulty. I cannot choose all my circumstances, but I can choose my attitude in which I deal with them. I choose to press on. There is a sentence that spoke to me that says "Obstacles are seldom the same size tomorrow as they are today." With that, I have some good news. I'm scheduled for an MRI next week to see how much things have progressed. Doctor says lymph nodes are barely detected and lump is significantly smaller. This is wonderful news, and I embrace it. We will have results before I start weekly treatments tomorrow, which will continue until November.

I think that one of the hardest things for me to do is to sit by and wait and not lose hope and stand strong while time goes by and remain quiet in my journey to conquer cancer. Life does go on for all of you and my family. I am living it through you every day. Please continue to stop by and visit and call and keep in touch. I will do my very best to stay in touch as well. This constant contact is uplifting and keeps me in the circle of life about your families and vacations and all that is good in your lives.

Okay, here's a funny story: One long warm day as I wait at home to make a trip anywhere, Glenn, Conrad, and I head to Home Depot. I have a short energy level so my trip is quick. We head back home and stop at 7-11 at 9:30ish at night. By this time, I'm overdone and hot. I proceed to take off my wig (I'm bald, remember), and sit in the front seat of the car. Conrad is sitting behind me, and Glenn is renting movies. :) Conrad says over my shoulder very cautiously, "Mom, you do realize that you don't have your hair on?" I say, yep, don't care, too hot! We both laugh because there are three teenage boys in the car next to us with some funny faces. I guess it's only hair, right?

Thank you all for everything you do, every day, to make others' lives worthwhile and in doing so enriching your own lives! I'm honored to have you as my friends. With love, Jody

CHAPTER 4

Round Two: Second Set of Chemotherapy, Update 1

Sent: Mon 9/12/11 11:28 p.m.

Unfortunately, there has been a delay in my update, and I apologize to those of you whom I do not see often. I was set to start my second set of chemo on Sept. 1. Glenn took me to Swedish that day, and for some reason (doctor says accumulated effects of chemotherapy), I could not pull myself together and wrap my head around starting another round of treatment. I was so emotional that I was in tears for my blood draw and could not stop them from coming. A wonderful nurse who tried to calm me down spoke of many things and ended with a hug. What a mess I was still and proceeded to sit with Glenn (he attempted to comfort me) and then on to my oncologist. The tears continued without fail. The nurse asked what I was feeling.

I said, "Tired, upset, and want to be done with this!"

She proceeded to tell me that I needed a week off to rejuvenate myself. I became more upset knowing I had to extend my treatment out another week, closer to Thanksgiving. I agreed that I was in no condition to start treatment. Glenn and I left. I felt relieved soon as we walked out the door.

I spent the next week outside and walking, trying to get back to a positive place of normal (whatever that is now) so I could start again next week. It was wonderful not to think about having cancer or treatment for a whole week!

I believe that the people supporting me had a better understanding of what I was going to go through. I was not prepared for the emotional roller coaster I would be on! Not doing the things I enjoy, like cooking, working out, volunteering, yardwork, taking kids all over town, and sports, was frustrating. I'm not the kind of person who sits around.

I think that going to chemotherapy and seeing all of the other cancer patients is taking its toll on me. I remain strong-willed and persistent, regardless. My eyes have been opened wider, and my heart is bigger. There are so many small things that make a huge difference to those who are receiving treatment. One person stands out. I never knew her name, but she smiled and saw my port with all the small tubes coming out and asked if it hurt. I said they numb it and she could also numb the area before she comes. This just gave her some comfort, knowing I'd been through it. She told me her elderly mother had just died three weeks prior of breast cancer and that she was diagnosed the day after her mother died with the same cancer. She asked me how I got my cancer.

I said, "They don't know, and nobody in my family has cancer."

She had already had surgery and a port and was starting chemo that day and staying overnight. I could tell she was scared and also that her cancer was serious. I told her I was not having a good day (through my tears) but somehow managed to tell her that it would be okay and to let the nurses know it was her first time. They were so wonderful and caring and would do everything to make her comfortable. She smiled and thanked me.

So many lives have been changed, including mine. By cancer and all of you. This is a very long and emotional road. I look forward to seeing all of your positive faces and hearing your loving and kind words. These things carry me through even when I want it to be over with each week on that drive to Seattle for another treatment. Those of you who are praying, please continue to pray for not just me but for my family. Challenging times but I have faith that we shall come through being better people and a stronger family.

Treatments are weekly on Thursdays. I've had two, with ten more to go! Feeling stronger most days and definitely better than with prior treatment schedule. I will have another MRI some time in October. Then after that, we discuss what type of surgery I will have. A week at a time is as far as I can go. Having school back in with three kids in sports feels wonderful yet overwhelming at the same time.

On a positive note: A dear friend from college is visiting this week and walking with me and going to treatment on Thursday. There is something about an illness that brings out the love we feel for others. It brings to the surface those feelings that we should always tell those important to us how much they mean, for we may not have another chance. With that, I want you all to know how much you mean to me and how important you have been throughout the years during the good times and struggles. I feel so fortunate to have so many wonderful people in my life. With love, Jody

CHAPTER 5

Strategies for Coping; Second Set of Chemotherapy, Update 2

Sent: Sun 10/02/11 11:22 a.m.

Four treatments under my belt, with eight more to go! Coping, in so many ways, has become my greatest challenge. I remain positive for Thursday's treatment. At least that's how it starts out. Glenn and I usually have a nice breakfast after getting the troops off to school. Make the drive to Seattle and the extra boost of adrenaline for coping kicks in.

First stop, check in and get slip for the lab. Head to the lab with slip and let them know I have a port and then sit and wait for my turn. My name is called, and I follow the nurse back to verify my name and birthdate. We exchange pleasantries while she numbs my port on my chest with a small needle. We discuss how many treatments I have while it's getting numb. She then inserts the access needle for treatment, which is U-shaped, into my port. This is uncomfortable but does not hurt. She takes blood to analyze my white blood count for my oncologist (whom I see next). She tapes it all to my skin and sends me on my way. I grab a candy on the way out to get rid of the yucky taste in my mouth from the alcohol (when accessing the port with the needle, saline is put through to be sure the path is clear. This can cause a taste of alcohol in the mouth).

I take the slip to the oncologist's desk and wait for a nurse (another one) to call me back. Glenn always sits and waits and asks me how it went. "Fine," I say. While we wait, I remain working on my positive self to cope with the next step. Nurse Betsy comes out with her smiling face to greet us and take us back for the scale to see what my weight is (ladies, this is no fun with your husband watching each week), then into the room for a blood pressure check. We discuss how my week went, how I've been feeling, what medications worked or not, and if we should change something. She looks up my blood draw information, which is usually good on the white blood count. This means that my body has recovered nicely. We talk about how many strands of eyebrows I have left and likewise on the eyelashes. Betsy always reassures me that I look great and it will all grow back. It keeps me upbeat for the time being. Coping with loss each week can be exhausting. Now, if it was weight loss, I'm sure I would feel differently! Who cares if that comes back?

Dr. Rinn, my oncologist, comes in after Betsy has given her the lowdown. It's never planned, but any one thing could trigger my behavior. Any question about how the kids are doing usually brings me to tears. Everyone reaches for the tissue box. I become frustrated with myself for breaking down while the doctor tells me that these things are all normal and reassures me that it's tough for everyone. I mention that I've called the social worker for advice. Also, I made an appointment for myself with the cancer physical therapy specialist for next week.

She is happy and says this will be very helpful for me with my aches and pains after each treatment. I smile, trying to compose myself and cope once again. She tells me I'm doing well and that we will order another MRI in the next couple of weeks, then we talk to the surgeon.

I say, "Am I done? Let's get out of here and get on with it."

She says, "Yes!" They both lovingly touch my shoulder as if to say, hang in there. Glenn and I head up to the third floor.

The third floor is where chemotherapy is done. Normally, I check in and ask for a room with a view. Today, I ask for a private room and a spa treatment. This always makes me feel better, and the person behind the desk smiles. Humor does help with coping! My name is called by a nurse, and we are escorted to my private room. I verify my name and birthdate, yet again, get comfortable in my recliner, and the nurse puts warm blankets on me for comfort. I grab my magazines and Zen music to relax and cope with what's next. Glenn asks if I'd like some juice. I usually say yes and ask him not to leave until she starts the anti-nausea meds. The nurse always asks if I want something to drink or a lunch.

Glenn and I usually discuss what he will be getting for lunch once I get started. He leaves briefly to get lunch to bring back (how does he cope?). Does he let it out in the elevator down or outside during his breath of fresh air? Or does he just keep it all inside and keep focusing on work? I always wonder how he's doing. He puts on a good face for me, but we are one, and I feel his hurt and frustration, knowing that making me comfortable is all he can do for me. He is strong and will hold it all together, at least in my presence. We all cope in our own ways. With Love, Jody

CHAPTER 6

Support Groups

Sent: Thur 10/13/11 7:25 p.m.

We discuss the possibility of making our support groups today. Glenn goes to a cancer caretaker group, and I have a living with cancer group. I know he won't say no, but he didn't really say he wanted to, either. Four and half hours later, we are still at Swedish. My treatment is done. Glenn has been sitting in my room, working on his laptop to get whatever he can done. The nurse removes my U-shaped needle and tapes me up, and we are on our way downstairs to the cancer center. I head to my group and Glenn to his. The support group is one and half hours. Mine was sort of like AA (like in the movies): "My name is Jody, I have stage 4 limited cancer diagnosed on June 2 of this year, on the second set of chemo every week until Nov. 17, then surgery to follow."

That's when I lost it; someone asked if I had a date for surgery, and I said through my tears, barely audible, that I could not think about it at this point. After that, I sat back and kept my mouth shut and listened to person after person; about ten of them do the same speech. I was amazed and brokenhearted and feeling so much compassion for these people and their ability to cope with a lot of the same things I was dealing with. Three of the people in the room were terminal. I just sat and cried for them, for me, for all of us. Once again, the tissue box was headed my way. I needed a towel or something.

After the meeting, I met with Glenn, who only gave me tidbits of information about his group. I could tell he was drained too. He mentioned that one of the ladies in his group just lost her husband and described how her life with him was. I cannot even imagine how emotional that room was. Six hours later, drained, we pulled our strength together for the ride home to cope and deal with the rest of life.

I feel thankful for my life and all the support we are given. Coping takes on several different aspects. I've spoken to my kids about this. We can cope by ignoring, cope by answering questions, cope by simple hugs, cope by offering help, cope by just crying or talking it out, or cope by focusing on someone else's hardship and assisting them. Whatever coping mechanism we use, as long as it's healthy, is okay. Life is going to be bumpy and challenging, but the method we use to cope will determine our strength and persistence for the next storm.

Love to you all, Jody

CHAPTER 7

The Active Program

Chemotherapy 3, nearing end of treatment:

Sent: Tue 11/01/11 5:50 p.m.

Lots of information, so let's get to it.

Had my third MRI last week. Findings: continued positive response to chemotherapy and decreasing in size. Also, appearance of the axillary lymph nodes also remains significantly improved since the initial exam on 6/15/11. No abnormal internal mammary lymph nodes are identified. This is all positive information!

Last week I started a new program called the "Active Program." This program is designed to help cancer patients stay active, however little activity, to remain strong during and after treatment. The doctor and physical therapy staff are wonderful and extremely supportive. My nurse has been asking for a while if I have tingling in my fingers or toes. Usually when she asks, it means that is what's coming next. Kind of like eyelashes and eyebrows! (They have since departed, as well.) In physical therapy, we are working weekly on balance issues because as treatment continues, my nerves in the feet and hands become numb, and I could have limited use. This is called neuropathy. This can be managed somewhat with physical therapy. I have to walk ten minutes per day and have home exercises, together with a weekly appointment.

Strength vs. energy: I've the strength of ten women, of course, but unfortunately, only a lightbulb worth of energy! It seems to go quickly. Because of the extended effect of chemotherapy, my production meter has significantly declined. I was relieved to know after talking to Dr. Zucker in the Active Program that this is normal. Dr. Zucker and his staff are strategizing and helping me conserve my energy when necessary and keeping track of the times when I can use more energy. Does that make sense? Somehow after reading his flier on ways to conserve energy, I realized that this is really becoming an issue for me. I went to Target with Glenn the other day. I was so exhausted that I could not put on any makeup or even get out of the car. I was so overcome with emotion that I chose to stay in the car and cry. Some days are just harder than others.

CHAPTER 8

Chemotherapy-Induced Peripheral Neuropathy

CIPN usually starts in the hands or feet and creeps up the arms and legs. Sometimes, it feels like a tingling or numbness. Other times, it's more of a shooting or burning pain or sensitivity to temperature. It can include sharp, stabbing pain, and it can make it difficult to perform normal day-to-day tasks like buttoning a shirt, sorting coins in a purse, or walking. An estimated 30 to 40 percent of cancer patients treated with chemotherapy experience symptoms of chemotherapy-induced peripheral neuropathy.

CHAPTER 9

Outside Support

Sent: Tue 11/01/11 5:50 p.m.

About three weeks ago, I realized that my eyelashes and eyebrows could no longer be seen. I was quite concerned and did not want to leave my house. I noticed a flier in the paper mentioning Ulta, a new store in the nearby shopping center. They had a picture of false eyelashes. I called and talked to Krista, the manager. I explained my condition and told her what I needed. I went down to the store the same day. Krista was a wonderful, supportive, loving, and kind soul, and she had worked with cancer patients before. She taught me to draw eyebrows, put on false eyelashes, and much more. I have since seen her three times. Each time, she has listened and helped with every detail and sent me off with a smile and a warm hug. What a lifesaver she was for me. She made me look pretty again and not feel like my face had disappeared. Which to me it had. I am so grateful. It's the small things.

Thursday, November 3, 10, and 17 conclude this round of chemotherapy! Friday, November 4, Glenn and I meet with my surgeon, Dr. Tierney, to discuss what type of surgery I will have and how much radiation after that. I'm not looking forward to this, as you can imagine. Great to have choices, but I wish there were some other way out! I know that the three of us will come to a conclusion that will be best for me. I will reach down deep for the strength, as in each step before this. One more step to my cancer being cured and moving on to what's next. Nobody really wants to make these choices, but somebody has to.

As the weeks ahead come to a conclusion, I ask for your prayers for myself and my family. Give us all the strength to endure what is ahead. Our family will spend the Thanksgiving holiday together away from home to rest, rejuvenate, and reconnect with each other. We have a lot to be thankful for.

I thank each and every one of you for your love and support throughout these past six months. We so appreciate the village that has stepped in and offered to do anything and everything. It really means so much. You all are amazing, wonderful, big-hearted folks, and we love you. With love, Jody

A funny: I was trying to make pasta after school for the kids, and the steam from the noodles ruins wigs (makes them frizzy), so without thinking, I took off the wig and threw it to the kids to catch so I could finish. Some big eyeballs with that move!

CHAPTER 10

End of Chemotherapy

Sent: Fri 12/02/11 12:34 p.m.

First, I want to let you all know how much your letters, cards, and meals have supported not only myself, but my family. I thank you from the bottom of my heart. Spending Thanksgiving being thankful for so very much and grateful for even more. You all mean so much to us. I really feel as though my life has been put on fast forward. It has been a month since I've updated you all. Been so busy with medical appointments and trying to sort it all out.

Finished chemotherapy on November 17 after twelve long weeks. Getting some energy back. This is really encouraging to me. Unfortunately, I've swelled like an oompa loompa. Sausage fingers, cankles, and puffy face. This is from chemo and will eventually go away! Hopefully sooner than later.

Spent the last couple of weeks with breast surgeon, plastic surgeons, and preparing for surgery, which we'd hoped to be this coming week. Little did we know how incredibly complicated this process would be. I've spent several hours researching lumpectomy versus mastectomy, trying to come to a decision that I could live with and would work with the surgeons involved. Backing up a bit ... spent the Thursday before Thanksgiving with the ultrasound tech. She was to mark the area for the surgeon to remove. Unfortunately, she could not see the affected area to mark it. This was upsetting to me because I knew the needle-marker was next with MRI direction if ultrasound was not successful.

Next day, Friday, went in for MRI procedure, and the doctor involved congratulated me, which was confusing. He said that it was wonderful that ultrasound could not detect affected area because this means that the chemotherapy has done its job! It was so hard to see, and they wanted to be precise with MRI. This was good news! Took me some time to absorb this good news. So then had MRI-directed marker placed. Whew, done with that!

The complicated nature of research and consultation with surgeons has left me with a decision that may be difficult to explain, but I will do my best. It was really my oncologist, who is a cancer survivor, who really gave some insight to Glenn and I.

She said, "You don't need to start with a mastectomy. Start with a lumpectomy [removing affected area only] with lymph node dissection."

Then a week later, pathology comes back to reveal if the area affected was all removed. If it is, we are done. If not, a second surgery is required to remove the remainder. If positive for removal, we are done. If not, then the next step is mastectomy. For me, this was a lot of ifs, not to mention a lot of surgeries.

Next choice: Start with mastectomy and get all affected area. Done. Left with scars that cannot be dealt with until after radiation. Healing after is about twelve months of recovery and a prosthetic. Plastic surgeon will not touch radiated area. Skin is damaged and not pliable. Didn't like this one, either.

Here is what I chose: By having reconstruction at the same time as breast surgery, the doctor will be able to take a much larger area around the affected breast, therefore eliminating a second or third surgery. In order to accomplish this, I have chosen a plastic surgeon who has successfully performed several of these surgeries with my breast surgeon.

Here is how it goes: This is an extremely long procedure and starts with breast surgeon. Approximately two to three hours taking out affected area with lymph node dissection, and then, while I'm still under anesthesia, the plastic surgeon does reconstruction on the affected breast and reconstructs the other to match. This will take approximately four to five hours. While I'm not entirely thrilled with this choice, I am sure this is the best decision for me. One surgery, all cancer gone, and wake up with a matched pair! Recovery is four weeks. I still have to have radiation, regardless. By choosing this process, it will alleviate the need for more surgeries. At this point, my emotional meter is not half-full, it's half-empty!

Since this takes an entire day in the operating room, the surgeons involved only had this date: December 20. While the offices involved tried to work together to get an earlier date, which my oncologist preferred, they were unsuccessful. I believe that everything happens for a reason. I have a head cold that just surfaced, so I will be taking care to heal before surgery day. I'm certain in my decision to have this team of highly successful surgeons taking care of me. (I've attached some information that may make things clearer about the process, should my information not be. It's a lot of information. Please don't feel obligated to read it.)

At this time, I am still a cancer patient, but I ask for your prayers so that a week later, when the lab results are returned (we are hoping to get results before the oncologist goes on vacation), that I will be a cancer survivor.

I really hope by sharing my journey through all of this that we shall all have a better understanding of the process of going through cancer treatment. I know that before this diagnosis, I can honestly say that I had no idea of what people have to go through. So while at times, I feel that it's too much information, I also feel it's necessary.

This is my story, and every story is different, even though it may be the same diagnosis. My aunt's story is different, your mother's story is different, a sister's story is different. When dealing with cancer, each person's journey is specific to them. We are all different people and have different concerns and outcomes. One thing that remains the same, though, is that we are all loving, compassionate, and caring individuals going through cancer, and we need love and compassion in return to keep going. This has been so important, and I thank each and every one of you. Our lives have all been changed. All my love, Jody

CHAPTER 11

Partial to Complete Mastectomy

Sent: Mon 12/05/11 2:53 p.m.

I will be having two surgeries as of today. I had a call from my oncologist late Friday after I sent the update out. She made some calls to surgeons and said that it cannot wait, so here we go! On Thursday, Dec. 8, at 6 a.m. arrival, and 8:30 a.m. surgery. This will be the dissection of lymph nodes and removing the affected area. I ask for your prayers that it's all removed so we can proceed with the other surgery on the 20th.

Sent: Friday, December 09, 2011 6:17 p.m.

Subject: Home from Surgery

Hi everyone! I'm home today from surgery at Swedish yesterday. I ended up staying overnight to get pain under control. I'm glad that I did. Surgery went well and was three hours or so. I have a wonderful surgeon. Had lymph nodes removed and a partial mastectomy. I'm extremely sore but otherwise I feel great. Glenn and April are taking good care of me. Mother-in-love will be coming up before my surgery on the 20th.

A side note: while waiting for the surgeon yesterday morning, the plastic surgeon came by and chatted with Glenn and I, then came back by and spoke to the surgeon about incision she wanted her to make on me, so they were on the same page. I feel very confident that I am in good hands. Thank you all for your prayers. With love, Jody

Sent: Wed 12/14/11 10:54 p.m.

Thank you all for your good wishes and prayers! It's with a heavy heart that I send this, but feel it's necessary. I was expecting to receive a positive call from my surgeon today so as to move on to Tuesday's surgery. Instead I received the following: "Good response to chemotherapy, removed margins marked and even tissue beyond to ensure clear response: Laboratory tests came back with margins that have evidence of infected area that remain, even after removing a huge margin area." I now prepare myself for a complete mastectomy on Tuesday instead of reconstruction. Hard to find something positive, but thank goodness we went this route before getting reconstruction. Heading to Seattle for postsurgery follow-up in the morning and to find out how Tuesday, December 20 will go. Warmly, Jody

CHAPTER 12

Pathology/Postsurgery

Sent: Wed 1/04/12 2:08 p.m.

Thank you all for your love, kind words, and multiple ways in which you support our family. We cannot thank you enough! Let's start with the clinical pathology report. I will try to keep it in an understandable form. I had a good but only partial response to chemotherapy, with scattered residual tumor deposit. This tumor reached out and multiplied over at least 4.5 to 5 cm area. This made for multiple positive margins, meaning infected area. Also, 2/26 lymph nodes showed residual tumor, with 1/26 showing treatment effect. While chemotherapy shrunk the nodes, they were still infected. This information was from the first surgery on December 8. The information meant that the surgeon did not want to take the chance to try to get the remaining infected tissue, but wanted to take it all to be sure that she got it all of it. Makes sense! December 20 was the second surgery for mastectomy to retrieve remaining infected tissue. Final pathology report after the surgery. (Residual microscopic foci of infiltrating ductal carcinoma, which means that under a microscope, these two foci measured 1.5 and 0.6 mm and surgical margins posterior (deep) and close (1.8 mm), which means that under a microscope, there is still evidence of this small margin, and close means close to but not penetrating the chest wall, meaning that radiation will be next to be sure that whatever is left will be annihilated, yet once again.)

The fight remains … sigh, day by day. I continue to get stronger. Hurray! I feel each step for the past several weeks, while difficult, has given me the strength to move forward. The time has not gone by without its moments. I will share a few in the hope that you will all feel as I have. Having human presence, touch, conversation, and love, together with faith, can move you to do things or get through moments you never thought you could. And to realize how incredibly important it is!

Preparing for surgery number #2 was simple, and I was ready. I already knew what to expect since I'd been there only twelve days earlier. Strong and confident until the anesthesiologist informed me that she could not find a vein. She continued to poke me with a needle, to no avail. What seemed like over and over until I lost it. Tears from this. I could not shake during the walk to the operating room. I was wanting to look strong for the person who loves me the most.

A funny thing: When I climbed up onto the bed and said hi to my surgical team, I said, "It smells like chicken in here." One of the nurses said, "I haven't heard that one before," and we all laughed. Someone asked my doctor if she had chicken for lunch, and she laughed and that's all I remember.

Surgery went well. The pain that I was having in my armpit from lymph node dissection from first surgery was alleviated by the doctor. She removed scar tissue, which she thought was causing the pain. Stayed overnight, which was the plan. I already knew what I was going to eat. It's funny how having someone else cook and bring food to you in bed can seem so glamorous. I am so thankful that Glenn was able to stay overnight with me and just be there. I was not prepared for the emotions I was going to have after seeing what had been done to me. I now had a bunch of skin sewn together. He was there to tell me that I would be okay and that we would get through this. Only a moment to feel this … not a lifetime.

As we prepared for the holidays and I was recovering, I had to have this drain that is attached to your armpit (lovely addition to any outfit). It was extremely painful and apparently touching the nerve, so on December 25, we headed to Swedish in Seattle for the doctor to check it out. Turns out it looked like it was getting infected. I was put on antibiotics, more pain meds, and I had a quick cleaning of the area. Another one of those moments. With Love, Jody

CHAPTER 13

Next Steps

Sent: Sat 1/14/12 2:46 p.m.

It was time to head to Nordstrom to be fitted for a camisole. I thought this was going to be simple. Two experienced ladies took me in the back room, and we had a conversation about what my choices were and what I needed. I had no idea what I needed. A camisole with a puff, for those of us who need a little more. These were some of the nicest ladies. One asked me if I'd like her to help me try it on or could I do it by myself. Well, I burst into tears, afraid of her seeing what was under my shirt. She held my hand and reassured me that she has seen a lot and been doing this for twenty years and it would be okay. Another moment.

Yesterday, the drain came out. What a relief. I feel one more step toward normal, whatever that may be now. Every time I leave Swedish in Seattle, I want it to be the last time. Why do I feel this way? I guess it means that it's over. Another moment for me to realize that it's still not over. Still taking pain meds and working toward stopping them altogether. Started back walking again. I know it's what I have to do. Tomorrow, I have my consultation for radiation therapy. I can honestly say that I am not looking forward to it. Another moment to deal with and move on from. Feels like life is a bunch of moments. I will not be defined by any one. They are not all trying moments, lots of happy beautiful ones, and I choose them to keep me focused. Signs of recovery are that my hair is beginning to grow. Scary crazy different color and uneven hair but, nonetheless, hair. Began Latisse [a product to help get those lashes back] and noticed last night that my eyebrows are showing signs of growth, although they look like those angry eyebrows since it's only in one place.

Thank you all for letting me share my experiences with you. These things are extremely difficult to discuss in person. I am stronger because of all of you. Please know that everything you do and say lifts me up every day! For that I am thankful. With love, Jody

CHAPTER 14

Stronger than Cancer
(Third Round)

Sent: Tue 1/24/12 1:39 p.m.

I continue to be grateful for all of you in my life. Please know that each of you have lifted me up always at the right time and when it was needed. You may never have even known the positive affect that your note, phone call, check-in by text, smile of encouragement had on me. Even in the most difficult of times, it has been hard to keep my emotions from showing. I treasure you all!

It's been twelve days since I had my follow-up with my oncologist after surgery. Even as I sit here alone, it is difficult to say: twelve more weeks of chemotherapy. This will be my third round. Bring it! It's one thing to know what you have to face but, it's another thing to come to terms with it. Not quite there yet. I had a feeling, since it was a late appointment on Friday the 13th! Chemotherapy starts tomorrow, 1/25. I'm not sure if I can describe how getting news of more chemotherapy felt. It felt like back in May on that late Friday night when Glenn was working out of town and I was the one on the telephone with the doctor who had to deliver the news to me that day that I had cancer. It feels devastating today. And how was I going to tell everyone? Well, I continue to ask for your prayers because I know everything happens for a reason.

A dear friend gave me this wonderful book called *Stronger than Cancer.* I leave you with some of the very meaningful quotes: "Courage comes and goes. Hold on for the next supply." "It takes each of us to make a difference for all of us." "We must accept infinite disappointment, but we must never lose infinite hope. "Having someone who understands is a great blessing for ourselves. Being someone who understands is a great blessing to others." Hang in there. Things fall apart so that things can fall together." Each of us has a spark of life inside us, and we must set off that spark in one another."

I discovered I always have choices, and one of them is a choice of attitude. I am stronger than cancer. With love, Jody

PS. Soon as I pull my bootstraps up, I will send a more informative update.

CHAPTER 15

Perseverance

Sent: Mon 2/13/12 3:31 p.m.

First, if you have called or written or have texted me and have not gotten a reply, I do apologize and have not done so for any other reason than just not wanting to talk about my situation. I appreciate you all so much and just want you to know that it's been a challenging few weeks starting that third round of chemotherapy. I remain strong. Some days, it just takes so much to pull up those bootstraps and put another foot forward. As I've thought about writing this update, many things come to mind.

1. Chronic pain and management: I know lots of people can relate to this on many levels. How do you express to those you love that you have this pain without feeling like it's complaining? I feel like my attitude has said it all! Not in a good way, either. It's quite easy to be nice when you're feeling okay, but when you're not, you can feel like nobody really understands. They want to, they want to help, and they love you.

2. Relationships: Life goes on, and you cannot hide from it. I have smiled when I've wanted to cry. I've counted to ten to keep from screaming. I've even tried ignoring things, hoping they would go away! The emotions of it all have really opened my eyes. I met a lady at Swedish recently who began speaking to me about what kind of cancer I had. Of course, I opened myself up to her questions, since I decided not to wear a wig or hat that day. She offered some of her journey while I sat and listened. She told how she had colon cancer and the doctors did not expect her to live. She told me about her fierce drive and courage. She had a lot to live for, and this kept her going. I'm not even sure how many rounds of chemotherapy she had; it was a lot. She was still here and moving forward. What had she been through? I could not even imagine. I felt as though she understood something about what was happening to me. She was kind, she was funny, and she even had some tips for my crazy-looking hair. I don't even know her name, but she said some things to me that day that I needed to hear. Thank goodness for her that day.

Met a couple while waiting for chemotherapy. Again, I guess my hair (or lack of it) meant that I had a story. Not sure how it started, but I found out that this man was getting chemotherapy for the first time and expected it to take five hours. As we exchanged information about where to eat and various other cancer-related items, I felt myself becoming emotional as my eyes welled up. I fought back the tears, and I know he and his wife looked directly into my eyes, knowing it was difficult. I was able to stay strong and show them that they could do this, just as we have. Eventually, it would be okay. We talked about ways of talking to others or writing about our experience. It's incredibly difficult to keep everyone up to date and put on a happy face. I don't know their names, either, but I hope that we were able to be their encouragement that was so important on that day.

3. Love: As I touch the front of my robe with my chin, I realize it's very moist. Love is the answer to a lot of things. Instead of telling you all of what I've gone through for the last three or four weeks, I choose to express my love and appreciation for all of you and everything that you do and continue to do to care for all of those around you. Most importantly your families, friends, and my family. We all have each other to lean on, support, encourage, and love. Just on the eve of Valentine's Day, so many things come to mind. I realize that when I think of encouragement and how important it is to each of us and our children and in our lives, that we must say it … at that moment; don't let it pass. Find a way to let those you love and care for, know that they are important and how much they mean. It feels so good to be on the receiving side, but it is so much more important to give this incredible gift.

I remain stronger than cancer and continue to fight the fight! I leave you with this; you may have already seen it, but I really like it:

May Life's Greatest Gifts Always Be Yours
Happiness. Deep down within.
Serenity. With each sunrise.
Success. In each facet of your life.
Close and caring friends.
Love. That never ends.
Special memories.
Of all the yesterdays. A bright today.
With much to be thankful for.
A path. That leads to beautiful tomorrows.
And dreams. That do their best to come true.

With love, Jody

CHAPTER 16

Compassionate Nurses

Sent: Mon 3/05/12 2:14 p.m.

Before I begin, I would like to express my deepest appreciation and gratitude for the village who continues to love and care for our family. I have just finished my sixth treatment of chemotherapy of this third round. It has been a slow uphill walk in slippery sandals, to say the least. I have not felt good since the first treatment. We have adjusted the anti-nausea meds weekly, and I am having them put in rather than taking them orally. This seems to be somewhat better. I was pleased a few weeks ago to find out that I would be receiving a massage for my aches and pains. This was wonderful, especially before chemotherapy. I did have one and then was informed that my insurance does not cover it.

Last couple of weeks have really tested my strength, hope, and courage. I've felt as though I could not keep on this path. Spoke to my family members and said some things that I would never have before this (I guess in my right mind). There were words that didn't taste good coming out of my mouth. Fortunately, they gave me some of my own advice. I was told to "think clearly before making that decision," and "that sounds like you're quitting or giving up; why would you do that?"

I told them it was my decision if I was going to stop being treated. This was the week I went to be treated and my doctor was on vacation. It was an emotionally exhausting day, not to mention that I could not discuss these feelings with my oncologist. Had to show and go through with it. Through my uncontrollable tears, I managed to get through it. Everything seemed to bother me. The needle to numb the port hurt. The needle put into the port hurt. Coping was as challenging as ever.

This week, the doctor returned, and I knew I had to have this conversation. It was a tough one, and I knew it would not be easy. Tried not to think about it before I was actually there. The more I tried not to, the more I thought about it, and the more upset I became. We had not even left the house yet. It was a long, emotional drive to Seattle. When we went in to see the nurse, she must have known how I was feeling. She touched my shoulder and my leg to comfort me while she talked about my treatment and how all the effects on my body were taking its toll on my entire system.

She explained that my bone marrow was recovering each week and that my blood counts were beautiful. My body in that regard was bouncing back. However, the emotional and physical toll are great, and at some point, I would have to skip a treatment. She also looked me in the eyes and said that I was being treated by one of the best oncologists around and that she would trust her with her own life, without a doubt. This treatment was the right thing to do, but it was tough. The doctor came in and touched my shoulder and squeezed my hand as

I cried openly, just knowing it was another challenge I would deal with. We talked about things I could do, and she asked me if I would like to skip this treatment and start back next week to give myself time to recover. I said no, I was already here, so let's do it.

Went to the third floor for chemotherapy. A wonderful nurse took me back and asked me a few questions.

I mentioned my state of mind, and she stopped and got down eye to eye with me and said, "Look at what you are wearing. This beautiful scarf tells me that you are trying really hard to carry on, and you are giving it all you got."

Of course, she reached for the tissue box and told me it was okay to cry.

"It's okay here," she said, smiling, "and now let it out."

This was huge for me. Even though I felt as though I did not have the strength, she assured me that I did in fact show that I did. She started my treatment and then left to attend another patient. When she returned, I was hot, so I took off my wig to reveal my wild salt-and-pepper hair. We talked about hair and eyelashes and Latisse. When the nurse returned again after checking other patients, she asked me if I would show my lashes and hair to another patient who was down and talk to her. I immediately said sure.

She led a woman over to me while I was getting treatment. I smiled, and she could see that my hair came back and my lashes too. I explained that Dr. Rinn was responsible for the Latisse program and that it was available to cancer patients. She smiled and was so happy to hear what I had to say. I told her about Ulta and the support there. She returned to her chair to start her treatment after thanking me. The nurse came to me and told me how wonderful it was for me to talk to her patient and that it really made her day. She thanked me over and over.

It felt good to be someone positive on a day when I did not feel very good. I just thought, *What if I had skipped my treatment that day?* It has become a challenge to cope on a daily basis. Feeling more physical and mental limitations. Being tired and having a limited amount of energy daily.

Somehow, being there for someone else at a time when we are not feeling so great and giving encouragement has a positive effect on one's well-being. Very uplifting. With love, Jody

CHAPTER 17

Spreading the Love

Thirty-nine days since my last update:

Sent: Mon 4/16/12 1:17 p.m.

> Wow, time sure does fly! I apologize for the delay. In order to send out an update, I must retrace my steps, which is healing but can be emotional. Before I begin, I want all of you to know how incredibly grateful our family is to all of you for your loving support in so many incredible ways! Our lives are forever changed, and with the challenges, there have been so many blessings. Someday, I may share the wonderful stories and people who have touched my life and I know will touch yours.
>
> I have now completed all twelve treatments of my third round of chemotherapy. How eleven months have come and gone. I do believe that the last round of treatment was the most challenging, with accumulated fatigue and illness. I was told of these things but chose to ignore them as much as possible and for as long as possible. On March 25 around 8 p.m., I realized that something was not to be ignored. I had symptoms of heart issues, so I went to the emergency room. It was a

Sunday night (bad idea). After four hours and several tests, it was determined that the medication I had to take (Xeloda) was causing esophageal spasms (chest pains, upper body pains, and I felt sick). Fortunately, I was given some nasty thing to drink, which eliminated the pain in about twenty minutes! I guess ignoring this was not the right thing to do. Lesson learned. Consequently, I've been drinking these two Maalox-type drinks for a week to keep food down. Finally, the doctor says, "You are done with this medication and have one more treatment." It is not worth all of this. I was having trouble eating. I slowly felt better.

I had my eleventh treatment, and while the nurse was sitting with me to do the push chemotherapy drug, which is administered over six minutes, she started talking to distract me. They have so many patients with different diagnoses that I'm sure they could not remember them all. So as she started to ask, I started to think back and remember my first round of treatment back in June of 2011. It was A & C, then second was Abraxane, and third was Navelbine, which she was giving me. As I talked, she listened. As she talked, I listened to her every word as she began to explain what I have been through and the courage and strength together with the perseverance that it takes to continue to press on through treatment. She explained everything that I had been going through, as though she understood it all. It's rare to have someone interpret how you are feeling and actually get it right. It gave me some reflection. I could not believe what I had been through until she laid it all out! I was so grateful for the insight and the caring way she explained my journey and acknowledged the struggle. What a gift she had! This I will never forget. As she flushed my port and took the access needle out, I noticed her name badge. Her name was Grace. This brings a tear to my eyes even now.

A joke: Earlier that morning, when getting my port accessed, the nurse promptly delivered this joke: Knock knock. Who's there? Tumor. Tumor who? Tumor treatments to go! With love, Jody

The Scarf

Anniversary at Salish Lodge

The Robe

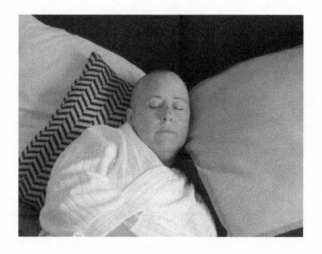

CHAPTER 18

Giving Hope

Sent: Mon 4/16/12 1:17 p.m.

I have a cancer care nurse provided by our health insurance. Her name is Michelle, and she calls every couple of weeks to check in and talk about whatever is on my mind and to give guidance and caring. I love her, but she always makes me cry, so there was a point when I did not want to talk to her. I was not feeling positive about where I needed to be mentally to continue. Then one morning, she found me! I'm so thankful she did. She reminded me about all of the positive things we had discussed earlier and what things I had told her were motivating me, like getting back to the gym. It is so far off that I could not keep that in front of me. She is wise and talked about some mental goals and short-term things that were within reach. In short, she put me back on track. This was huge! I start over every day, and this is the way! Leave yesterday behind, and anticipate all the good that is waiting tomorrow.

Yesterday was so rewarding. Let me explain. I wanted to remember this day, since it was the last treatment. Not just that, all of the wonderful people involved in my care. I decided to take one of my many journals to have them sign their names and department so that I would remember them all. I started in the lab with the jokester. She had a joke for today, which unfortunately, I'm unable to share in this setting. She congratulated me on being done and was happy to sign my book. I handed her a dark chocolate, which revealed a positive affirmation on the wrapper. She sent me off with a big smile and a hug.

Something I forgot: As I was waiting to go into the lab, a mother and daughter (about ten or eleven years old) sat down and began discussing if the daughter wanted to go into the lab with Mom. The daughter explained that it was extremely hard to watch. I could not help overhearing them, so when the mother asked for a drink of water, I promptly volunteered to show her where it was. I could tell her mother was weak and frail from her treatment but still smiling to be strong for her daughter. I could relate. When her daughter returned, she thanked me, and that is where the conversation began. I retrieved two chocolates from my bag, held out my hand, and delicately placed one in each of their hands while holding them. I explained with a smile that today was my last treatment and that I had been coming for eleven months.

I wanted to share this moment with everyone who was here who would listen. To let them know there is hope, and I'm proof. We had a wonderful conversation about hair and wigs and types of cancer. Many things that are important to cancer patients are hard to discuss outside of those walls. My heart broke as she told her story. I assured her that she was in the right place, with many caring souls to guide and support her. When she left, she thanked me for talking as I reached out and touched her arm so carefully. What a wonderful feeling to give hope, love, and caring!

Next, on to my oncologist and my nurse. Short visit today. Doing well and tolerating treatment. Four to six months to recover from treatments of eleven months. Don't rush it. Talked about radiation starting in two weeks. Fatigue involved and very tiring. Talked about long term-medication for hormone blocker. She ordered bone scan for osteoporosis. They both smiled and congratulated me for completing all treatments (did not take any breaks). I felt good. Got my ticket for treatment and mentioned my journal. They each gave me a big hug, and I thanked them for everything they have done. I reached out to both with my chocolate candy and held their hands and thanked them again. These are not just doctors and nurses. These are people with big hearts. Such loving and caring individuals who can make a person's day with just a smile.

Headed up to chemotherapy floor to check in. Gave the check-in gal a chocolate and explained why. She was so happy as we exchanged smiles. For some reason, I was the only person in the waiting room. Strange, since it's usually full. The nurse came out and escorted me back for my treatment. I mentioned it was my last. After I sat down, she apologized for not having a window seat today for my last day. I was going to be happy anywhere today! As word spread among the staff, each person came by to offer their congratulations and support. These people were my support system. When they ask how you were feeling or how you were doing, they expected the truth and genuinely gave their advice with love. They could tell when you were not being truthful. I guess it shows. I had come to know that it is a safe environment, despite what I was feeling.

As I ate my lunch, I knew I had a bigger purpose today. Not sure what it was. Record timing today for treatment! Have never gotten done in two hours. Glenn kept asking what I wanted to do to celebrate. I did not know. My journal was being sent around the floor for signatures. While packing up and having several conversations with hugs and appreciation, I spent time holding each nurse's hand, hoping to spread the love to all of the other patients being treated. What an amazing moment for all of us! I wanted them to know how important they all are to me and my family and the numerous people who will come after me. I asked if there was some rule about talking to other patients. The head nurse said I could talk to whomever I liked.

She also mentioned that there was a new patient today with her spouse and pointed in their direction. Without even a thought of what I was going to say to them, I headed over. I reached into my bag of chocolates and handed them out, with my simple explanation and my hands to offer comfort. I listened as Michelle and her husband told their story and mentioned their beautiful little girls. She asked a lot of questions about many things to come. I offered what I knew and assured her that she was going to be taken care of and that she was in the best place.

She told me she interviewed three oncologists and asked me who mine was. When I said Dr. Rinn, she smiled and said that is who she chose. She also explained how she had the genetic gene for the specific cancer and asked me if I had it and if I had to have my female organs removed. I said that I did not.

I looked her in the eyes and said with a smile, "We do what we have to."

It was going to be a long road for her and her family. I wish I could do more. We both offered our phone numbers and other information. We let them know that they could call either of us anytime for any reason. Wonderful couple in a whirlwind of information searching for answers. I hope they do call.

Moving on. A friend recently said that he and his wife were concentrating on building relationships. I haven't forgotten this comment; it has stuck with me. This has been such an important part of life for me. Every relationship we have is to be nurtured and savored. We are all stronger because of the relationships we have, not the things. I treasure each and every one of you. Never underestimate the strength, wisdom, and love that we can use to uplift each other through the good days and the challenging ones.

Thank you so very much for your continued support. With love, Jody

CHAPTER 19

Radiation Begins (ABC Therapy)

Sent: Sat 5/26/12 2:20 p.m.

Subject: Radiation Begins

Before I begin, I would like to express my deep appreciation for all of the wonderful people who are supporting our family in so many ways. We thank you from the bottom of our hearts. We could not do many things without all of you! Know that you are loved, and we feel the love you share each and every day. If you have sent an email or message or phone call or are trying to reach me, and I have not gotten back to you, please accept my apologies. You are on my list. In a good way, that is! Began radiation at Swedish in Issaquah on Tuesday, May 1. I have thirty-three treatments, Monday through Friday only. I'm going to explain the amazing process of my particular radiation therapy.

It is called ABC Therapy. ABC is a noninvasive, advanced technology that helps the patient hold her breath while she receives radiation therapy. Active Breathing Coordinator is one of the advanced radiation therapy technologies available at three Swedish Cancer Institute locations: Swedish/First Hill, Highline Medical

Center, and Swedish/Issaquah. ABC provides patients with left-sided breast cancer maximum protection from radiation to their hearts. Why is this technology important? In preparation for any radiation therapy, a radiation oncologist will use CT images of the tumor to prepare a customized treatment plan. The goal is to precisely target the entire tumor with the highest, most appropriate dose of radiation while limiting the amount of radiation to the surrounding healthy tissue and organs. My tumor has been taken out, so the purpose is protecting the heart. With left-sided breast cancer, the heart moves when the patient breathes. The heart is part of the healthy tissue that needs to be protected. Studies have shown that patients who have received large doses of radiation to some parts of their hearts or who have had large areas of the heart exposed to smaller doses of radiation have a higher risk of developing radiation-induced heart disease. How does ABC work?

When Active Breathing Coordinator is used during radiation therapy, the patient takes a deep breath before the beam of radiation is delivered. This deep breath increases the distance between the area receiving radiation (the breast tissue or chest wall on the patient's left side) and the heart. Increasing this distance means there is less risk the heart will receive any incidental radiation during treatment, and therefore, there is less risk of the patient developing radiation-induced heart disease. The ABC process begins with a referral and consultation with a radiation oncologist. After the initial consultation, the process includes the following:

Planning: The patient is first scheduled for a planning/training appointment, so CT images can be taken and the patient can become comfortable with the equipment and with holding her breath for a short period of time. As part of the planning/training appointment, the doctor and patient discuss the ABC procedure and determine the amount of time the patient will hold her breath. Usually a breath hold is just twenty to twenty-five seconds; however, the patient is always in control and can signal that she wants to resume breathing at any time if she cannot hold her breath for that length of time.

A small clamp is placed on the patient's nose to avoid accidental breathing through the nose. The patient also holds a mouthpiece, which is attached to a breathing tube, between her teeth. When the patient is ready, she takes a deep breath. When she has breathed in enough air to inflate her lungs to a predetermined volume, she holds her breath. A small valve in the breathing tube closes so no additional air can enter her lungs during the breath hold. This stops any movement. A clock in the treatment room allows the patient to see the time remaining. If at any time the patient wants to take a breath, she releases pressure on a switch, and the valve automatically opens so she can breathe. Typically, the deep-breath hold procedure is repeated four to six times during each treatment.

I could not have explained it any better. I start each day new. After twelve treatments, already I am doing well. Tight skin and red. A bit more tired but functional. I have learned so much about myself and other people during this process. There is an older couple I see every day; the wife is being treated for brain cancer. Jim and Linda have been married for fifty-two years. Yes, I said fifty-two. She is brave and so adorable, and we stay positive on the craziest things.

Since the radiologists only see my pants and shoes (wear hospital top for treatment), I decided to see how many different pairs of shoes I could wear to keep them interested, and it gave me something to focus on. It kept the other patients happy too. I had my toenails painted, and we all had something to talk about other than what we really were thinking.

Once a week, I see the doctor before treatment, and his first question is always, "What have you noticed?"

The first time, I said, "The drive." Got a funny look for that. Asked the nurse if I could dye my hair any other color. She said that it won't take and not to worry, that it will be changing colors on its own. It's coming in black and white, and for those of you as old as I, it looks like pin curls! Tight, crazy, curly. Nobody recognizes this. Not even me. I called my eighty-year-old grandmother the other day and told her that I had hair just like hers. She laughed.

During this phase of treatment, I'm really trying to focus on the blessings and stay positive, even when the challenges occur. There was a day during treatment when there were some issues. Breathing and holding in air were challenging because of allergies. I was on the table for an hour for a treatment that should only have taken twenty minutes. I became frustrated. I asked them to remove the monitor and closed my eyes. I told myself, *You can do this*, as the tears were rolling down my cheeks. The tech staff is phenomenal! They were apologetic, even though it was not their fault.

With love, Jody

CHAPTER 20

Health and Beauty

Sent: Sat 5/26/12 2:20 p.m.

I may have mentioned in a previous update a wonderful, adorable gal who works at Ulta. She has been instrumental in her support of my physical appearance, and she has a loving personality. She recently phoned me and said that she wanted to help other people going through cancer treatment with their hair loss and makeup. She didn't want them to have to go through what I did to find her. I said I would talk to some folks and get back to her. She was accepted with open arms, and in addition to working at Ulta, she will be volunteering at Swedish twice a week on her days off, educating patients and bringing her positive personality to those who need it.

In an effort to stay strong physically, I've incorporated large amounts of protein into my diet. In doing so, it has kept the sweet tooth at bay. This has allowed me to eat less and lose those unwanted chemotherapy pounds. This brings me to another incredible gal with a huge heart, who is so smart and continues to work hard. She has been working on a breast cancer diet app. She researched and found out that not all cancers are alike and that there are some foods that are better than others, and some food that should be avoided. She made an app for it. As sales on it progress, the plan is to donate 10 percent of proceeds in my name to a foundation of my choice. Incredible. I am so touched! It was just released on Android, Nook, Amazon, Blackberry, and she's trying to get it on iPhone. More information to come on this!

Recently, after being treated for so long, it has occurred to me that I have missed out on so many things and continue to do so. Most days, my logical self assures me that my time will come, and it's all for a reason. I have moments when impatience sets in, and anger and hurt try to take over. It's a roller-coaster ride. I swallow my tears, knowing that I'm still on the ride, and it will be some time before I can get off.

A while back, I finally had the nerve to go to the grocery store without my wig. I've shopped there for thirteen years. Needless to say, I could not hide any longer and had to face the questions. I was ready. I was met with smiles and warm conversation. One person asked about my short haircut, and I had to explain. It was hard, but she touched my arm and held my hand and understood. Then she told me a story of someone in her family and how cancer touches people of many different economic backgrounds. I did it! Caring and compassion made it easier, and she said that she would keep me in her prayers. I just got in the car and cried. There is so much good. I feel so grateful.

There is something that sticks in my mind that happened yesterday while at Swedish in Issaquah. There was a middle-aged man caring for his ailing mother. I've spoken to them both but did not know her condition. I asked him how his mother was doing. He replied that the scan she had yesterday revealed the extent of infected areas. She has decided to discontinue treatment at this point. I was shocked and told him how sorry I was. We both smiled in support, and I told him to take care and that I would talk to her when I saw her. I wished I could do more. Somehow, conversation with strangers is often uplifting in unimaginable ways. Does that makes any sense?

Good news: Had a bone scan for osteoporosis. It came back negative. So only fourteen or so more treatments of radiation are necessary. I'm told my skin is holding up well. Unfortunately, this will change before it gets better.

A funny: One of the technicians was getting me ready for treatment, and the breathing apparatus gets put in my mouth, and my nose is plugged. The other day, I was not paying attention, and the nose plug was coming at me, and I opened my mouth. The tech almost fell on the floor with laughter. It was very funny. I guess you would have to picture it.

Having so many positive relationships continues to change my life. You are all so incredible and appreciated in more ways than you will ever know. With love, Jody

CHAPTER 21

Radiation Rocker

Sent: Mon 8/13/12 4:04 p.m.

Time sure flies. My apologies for the long delay. I appreciate all of you so very much. Thank you for always being there with love.

Had my last radiation appointment on June 15. The last of the treatments go like this. Five remaining regular treatments. Eight more on just the chest wall, and the last five are on the incision area only. The reason for the last five is that there is a higher risk of reoccurrence in the less-well-oxygenated area. During this time of continued assault on the area in which my skin began to not only peel and blister, it became difficult to sleep and keep the irritation under control.

I remember one day in particular. I was on my way to treatment; it was Friday, and something stressful was going on with one of my kids. I had to call on a friend to discuss the situation to calm me down so that I could make it through that day of treatment. This was an important moment of reflection. Knowing how to reach out for help and going to the right person will bring you back around and guide you through. We all need people like this in daily life to keep us grounded: loving, supportive, understanding, sympathetic, and problem-solvers.

Until this day, I had made it through every appointment in Issaquah with a smile and positive outlook. I was having a breakdown of unacceptable (in my eyes) proportions. I knew I could not go in and face the lobby of patients in this condition. I parked the car and closed my eyes and let it all out! Why are we so hard on ourselves? I believe that strength and courage resonate with others. We all need a positive force to follow, even on our darkest days.

Fortunately, life hit the fast forward button, and concentrating on my issues took a back seat to preparing for two proms, two downhill races, a baseball tournament, camp, high school graduation, and a party, together with guests from out of town. This reminds me of a commercial I once saw. Something like "Life's events continue, even during cancer treatment." We are not just being treated but trying to do everything else at the same time. These events kept me busy and left little time to reflect on what I was actually going through.

On the last day of radiation, a special friend drove me and brought along a video camera. Wow. June 15: what a day to take it all in. I was met this last morning by the incredible staff I'd seen every day. This day, I introduced my friend, who would be recording the day's event. Lots of smiles. We took pictures with the folks who had been taking care of me for six weeks. Had my treatment, and came out to the lobby to celebrate. They had sparkling cider and some gifts and cards. Also there were the couple who had been there for all of it, Jim and Linda. Jim met me with a lovely plant and card. He congratulated me and wished me the best. We supported each other. As a spouse, it was difficult for him to see his wife going through treatment. I was able to understand some things about the importance of a supportive spouse and know that I should be empathetic to Glenn. The anxiety and pain all woven together with love for a person who is hurting. The spouse cannot do anything to relieve it. I know now that this is a difficult and helpless feeling. He was certainly put in my life just at the right time. It must be challenging to love someone through the pain.

I'm so thankful for all of you. You need to know that each of you played and continue to play such an important part of our lives. We all need each other. This enriches our lives. Here was the highlight point of the morning: In my medical gown in front of the close circuit television (which did not record, thankfully), I performed a dance for the entire staff to "I'm Sexy and I Know It," emphasizing "Girl, look at that body." It was the best! We all laughed and enjoyed the moment. I was so tired. I had worked on this dance at home all morning. It definitely left a memory with all of them and hopefully did not scar them for life.

With love, Jody

CHAPTER 22

Moving On

On June 14, I had my follow-up appointment after treatment with my oncologist, Dr. Rinn. This appointment went well. I will be taking a hormone blocker drug for the next five years. It's similar to Tamoxifen but called Letrozole. A friend took me to this appointment, and a second set of ears is always a good idea. The doctor discussed many things, some of which I did not understand, like not having a lot of energy for several months while my body is recovering from all of the chemotherapy, surgeries, and radiation. This will take a lot of patience (not one of my stronger areas). Even though I am all done, I cannot expect to get back to my life like it was before cancer.

After this visit, I had some unfinished business to take care of on the third-floor treatment center. There was a special person who was on vacation when I finished chemotherapy, and I was not able to say goodbye and let her know how much she meant to me. I made my way to the area, trying to figure out the right words to express my feelings. I saw her with a patient. As I waited for her to finish, she turned and caught a glimpse of me and smiled. I remembered this smile from every week of treatment and her open arms to soothe my fears and her gentle eyes that reached out with the love in her heart to make a difference to me.

Whatever I was feeling was okay to discuss in her presence. No judgment. The one person who could read me like a book, no matter how hard I tried to hide it. She was able to draw things out that I otherwise would not reveal to anyone. She had an honest and straightforward gift and a realistic view of how treatment can take its toll on you, emotionally and physically.

When she did come out, we exchanged a warm embrace, and all I could get out was, "Thank you so much for everything."

Somehow, she knew again how I was feeling. Her look to me was that it will be all right now. I did it! I will never forget you, Marilyn! You are an angel.

CHAPTER 23

A Year Later

Sent: Wed 09/19/12 2:41 p.m.

In the weeks following, I had to have a mammogram and met with a reconstruction surgeon. I've had so much done that my mind never does get time to go to the "what ifs."

Example: I had a mammogram and was told to wait for the results. What? Since when do we do that? Well, after cancer, apparently. Suddenly, these what-if feelings struck me like a knife. It felt like the longest ten-minute wait ever! All clear was the result.

I found a massage relaxation therapist. I have had three treatments, and I can say that little by little, my pain and range of motion in my left arm are improving. Unfortunately, my skin feels like it has been pulled up my armpit and wrapped around my neck tight. In preparation for reconstruction, I need to put castor oil on the area and work on stretching my arm. My doctor suggested swimming. In preparation for this, energy is needed, and lots of it. My mind is ready to get started, but it may take a little bit more to convince my body. I am getting there.

Yesterday, I had my first haircut in a year! Another friend of mine referred me to this wonderful caring gal who has experience in chemo hair and all that it encompasses. She cut off all my clown curls, with no guarantee that they will not return. My hair is short but is very cute and takes no time or effort. I feel like this is a small step back to normal. It feels so good. Like no hair and clown hair, it will take some getting used to. It's all good, though.

I want you to know that I think of you often. I am slowly reaching out to each and every one of you. I cannot forget the many things that have encouraged me and uplifted my spirit, together with the enormous amount of love for my family. Know that you have made a difference in the lives of others in ways that you may not have even imagined. When I think of all the folks who have given, listened, and supported me, physically, mentally, and emotionally, my heart is full, and my mind is overwhelmed. There is so much good.

Thanks to all the support of my friends, family, and medical team, I've celebrated another birthday and another wedding anniversary! Love to you all until next time, Jody

Sent: Tue 12/04/12 2:21 p.m.

Before I get started, I wanted all of you to know just how much I appreciate your love and caring attitudes throughout my recovery. I'm so thrilled to see each and every person. It helps keep us connected as I get better every day. Seeing you shows that I am another step closer to getting things back to order. I was instructed by my plastic surgeon to start swimming. I spent a month exhausted and thinking about it. I managed to make it once. Yes, once, and it took everything I had to get there. I was sore and felt like I tore my skin. Unfortunately, I did not want to hamper my recovery and not be ready for surgery, so that was it for swimming.

I've spent the last few months working on getting back to healthy. Saw a wonderful gal for massage therapy twice a month. This was a great addition to walking and preparing for surgery. Carol was able to loosen a lot of scar tissue, and I was able to gain movement in the process. In order to have a full understanding of what was needed, it was important for me to share my experience and story. This may sound like more than most of us would do (including me), but as a health care provider and someone who spends their career helping people feel better, they need to know. Withholding information results in inadequate treatment and unnecessary pain. When you're in pain already, this is very important. A relationship was formed, and new treatment and different areas worked on for relaxation. It was an enlightening experience, and I know she will help many others from the treatments explored on me as a cancer survivor. I will always have a special place in my heart for Carol.

With love, Jody

CHAPTER 24

Time Away

During the past few months, I felt as though I needed to spend as much time as possible with the people who are most important to me. I was able to get away for a couple of days to Discovery Bay over on the San Juan peninsula. I felt like a child again, looking at jellyfish and starfish in the clear waters with my dear friend April and just not thinking about a lot of the medical things to come. So much fun doing nothing but creating memories I will never forget. Over Thanksgiving, forced all three teenagers to sit in a car for ten hours to take the oldest to college. We spent family time like we haven't in a long time! We sang together, joked, and played games from the past. This is the kind of stuff moms keep in their heart to remind them that their kids really do like each other! Memories are what is important with loved ones. These are the things that keep me going, along with all of your kind hearts.

CHAPTER 25

Reconstruction Ready

Sent: Thur 12/06/12 10:21 a.m.

As I get ready for reconstructive surgery, there is a lot on my mind. Trying to remind myself that this surgery is different. The last two were removing the cancer, and now we reconstruct what was lost and move forward. I feel like my mind is clearer and that I am more aware of the process. I have a different plastic surgeon. She is wonderful and has been down this exact road, which I feel is a bonus. Surgery is this Friday, December 7, at 10:30 at Swedish in Seattle.

The plan: (1) Remove the Port-a-Cath on the right side of my chest (this is where all the chemotherapy drugs were given; it is connected to an artery directly to my heart). (2) Reduce the unaffected breast on the right side an entire size to match the reconstructed side. (3) The left side muscle (latissimus dorsi flap) uses muscle, fat, and skin from the back tunneled to the mastectomy site and remains attached to its donor site, leaving blood supply intact. This means they will move this muscle from my back under my skin to the front for a breast mound that will provide muscle and tissue necessary to cover and support a breast implant. (4) A tissue expander will be placed under the skin above the muscle to stretch the healthy skin to provide coverage for a breast implant. The skin currently there has been radiated and may not be suitable, but the surgeon will decide during the procedure if she needs to graft healthy skin from my back to accommodate the area for a healthy healing result.

Over the next four to six months after placement of the expander, I will have many office visits to slowly fill the device through an internal valve to expand the skin. Two weeks after surgery is the first expansion and every one or two weeks, depending on how the wound has healed. After the determined size is reached, then we wait a minimum of three months to let the skin and muscles settle. Then a second surgical procedure will be needed to replace the expander with an implant. I apologize if this is too much information. I would love to go in and return home with a new breast; unfortunately, it is not that simple.

During the surgery and in the coming weeks, I would ask for all of your prayers for my family. This is especially important for my spouse, who has to go with the flow and be positive when he is at my side when it's all over. I cannot imagine his thoughts or fears during this time. This will be a six-hour surgery, the longest so far. I know it is all a step forward, but there are things to endure that will certainly not be pleasant in the short term. I intend to stay strong and know that there is a reason for everything.

In the meantime, I want to leave you with the incredible song that brought me to tears. It expresses so much to all of you who mean so very much to me. It reflects the love you have given through your prayers, calls, letters, texts, food, and gifts of listening and caring. I feel it every day and am so grateful. Lots of love, Jody

Here it is: Celine Dion, "Because You Loved Me"

CHAPTER 26

Recovery

Sent: Sun 8/11/13 12:19 a.m.

Let me start by saying, has it really been eight months already? Three steps forward and two steps back. Surgery went well. It took everything I had for recovery. My body was working stealth overtime! All the surgery areas focused on have healed and were not without discomfort, and a ton of just keep on keeping on. I decided to try to focus on physical therapy and wellness during the expansion process to rebuild my left breast. I went every week, then every other, then after the sixth expansion, I decided I could no longer continue with the pain. Injections into my left side, while increasing the size to match my right reduced side, became unbearable. After hitting the muscle and back spasms continuously, I could no longer tolerate the pain meds or the pain.

My wonderful doctor, who has been through this process herself, told me she knew exactly what I was feeling and that she completely understood. While we discussed our feelings and thoughts on the process, it was decided that since I was there, I should get one last injection to stretch the skin. I didn't really want to; however, I could reconcile it, knowing this would be it. I would be done. Closed my eyes and prepared for whatever would come. Doctors always feel bad when they make you cry. Knowing she understood what I was going through made me feel better. I wasn't just a baby and deciding to give up.

She hugged me and said, "You are finished with this!"

I managed to make it through seven expansions over five months. During this whole process and in between expansions, I continued to go to physical therapy. Keeping movement in my neck and arm muscles was instrumental in succeeding. The positive reinforcement from my physical therapist as to range of motion gave me hope and strength to get through.

I realize that there are multiple elements when overcoming frustration, fatigue, and pain. Not everyone understands, and that's okay. I know how I'm feeling. Every single positive gift, whether verbal or physical, no matter where it comes from, keeps your light shining, prevents it from dimming, and provides motivation to face the next obstacle. There were many. Knowing there were some setbacks on the way and expecting them kept me focused to keep my eyes on the prize.

With love, Jody

CHAPTER 27

Strength

In this case, the prize was wellness and strength. Frustration sometimes took over, and I spent weeks at a time resting in between every errand, every chore, and what felt like every minute of every day, just to make it through. I knew something had to change. I needed energy, not just supplements, to get off this couch, and stat! That's when I discovered Nutribullet. Two doctors offered all of the nutritional information in a book that I could follow. I wanted this to be the answer. I needed to get moving again. It was difficult being patient with the process since my tolerance level ... well, let's leave it at that. This was something I could do for life! I gave myself two weeks to see if it made a difference. I spent every night reading and educating myself.

About eight days into it, I knew something was different. I began to feel purpose and awareness. These were the first steps for me to begin recognizing the health benefits that soon became a clear path on the road to recovering from my chemotherapy brain fog! As the weeks progressed, I improved and started feeling better, with some energy. I was in. Food and vitamins just were not enough to jump-start my system from overload back to ground level. If I feel good, I can do anything! It's been two months now.

Had my follow-up oncologist appointment and blood draw. Doctor said it wasn't just good; it was excellent. Glenn and I rode our bikes from home to Woodinville and back, some fourteen miles! I'm so proud that I could accomplish this. I am the master when it comes to overdoing it.

CHAPTER 28

Emotional Journey

Sent: Mon 11/18/13 02:19 p.m.

In December, I will have surgery to take out the expander and put in an implant. During this process, some tissue from my abdomen will be injected above where the implant is going. This is due to during the mastectomy, tissue was removed down to the bone above the breast. Injecting your own tissue stimulates the area to heal while making it look more natural. As we go through daily life, there has been an awareness with so many affected by cancer. I'm still affected by the scars, baldness, and other symptoms that I witness by those going through treatment. Having been through it, I still am unable to figure out what to say to others, but in my heart, I can relate. Not sure if I'm upset by what I see or what I'm feeling inside. This reminds me that we do not have to be defined by our struggles. We may have become stronger in ways that we don't even realize.

I was recently asked what I would be doing next? Couldn't go there and had to excuse myself from the room. I read somewhere recently that "when you are able to discuss what you've been through without upset, only then will your path become clear." While I have recovered substantially on the outside, I believe the emotional piece may take a bit longer.

As the days pass and I am integrated back into family and community life, I realize just how incredibly thankful we are to have the relationships and support. Each and every one of you played a part in lifting up our spirits. As I look around my home, I am reminded of that love in so many things. My heart is full. The Beatles said it best: "All We Need Is Love."

I look forward to the coming months, as I am feeling better. I am very excited to reconnect with so many of you and catch up on your lives. I will be in touch. Warmly, Jody

CHAPTER 29

Marching on to Wellness

This update is three years out after being treated with chemotherapy and radiation for stage 4 breast cancer. I hope this was informative and provides hope and encouragement to those who need it. First, I would like to start out with how incredibly blessed I have been. My faith has gotten me through many struggles. In April of 2015, a friend and I decided to start walking three miles a day, five days a week. Didn't really know for how long. What I did know was that being outside and being active at whatever I was able to do would be of benefit. It has been quite the journey the last eleven months, and today, I feel that I am able to share.

Calculating three miles a day, five days a week, for eleven months brought me to 660 miles walked. The tread on my shoes has the evidence of wear. My friend brought it to my attention yesterday, saying that her shoes were wearing out. What an "aha" moment for us both. This has not necessarily been a journey of purpose but a journey of wellness. We began walking in April, and for the next five months, there was no change in my physical health.

Let me explain: After walking each day, I would return home to rest for approximately the next two hours from being extremely tired. After four months of this and gaining weight, I believed that some energy would return. I sought out a naturopath in Seattle, Dr. Dan. He was wonderful and encouraging. He did, however, set me up with a ton of supplements at three times per day. I was following his prescribed plan and still felt like there was no change. He wanted me to go see a stress specialist and asked if I was depressed. What? No, I'm discouraged, not stressed or depressed. I considered his suggestions and even spoke to his suggested therapist on the phone. She agreed with me that I did not need stress counseling. The only stress I was having was that I thought I was doing the work and having no results. He encouraged me to keep walking.

I met with him every two weeks for three months. He suggested intravenous vitamin therapy to jump-start my body and said that the chemo and radiation can do a lot to my body and it would take some time to recover. I considered the intravenous therapy, which was not covered by insurance. I felt that the two hours getting it would bring me back to chemo days, and I could not go there. Had to press on to wellness. Dr. Dan kept me going and with humor, as well. I spent months getting on the scale in his office, only to have it increase every time! I was so frustrated. He began telling me that he would write down whatever number I wanted. Funny guy. I mentioned my thyroid, which is why I originally went to him to find a solution that did not involve more medicine.

To keep my cancer away, since it was hormone-fed, I take a hormone blocker for the next ten years. This actually began right after treatment. So after all the treatment and my hair, eyebrows, and eyelashes growing back, I couldn't be happier to get back to some kind of normal (which at the time I did not realize would forever be different). I began to lose my hair yet again! The doctor assured me that it would taper off; this was due to the hormone blocker. Handfuls and spots of no hair began to show. I was heartbroken but told myself that it was just part of my journey. I would look at pictures of how full and beautiful my hair used to be. New normal. I began to suspect that my thyroid was the culprit for a lot of the symptoms I was having. My general practitioner and oncologist both told me my levels were normal. Spent months looking at symptoms and long-term effects of chemotherapy and radiation. Apparently, radiation can harm the thyroid. My GP suggested I start taking Synthroid, and it would help. My oncologist concurred. However, after reading about the side effects, I did not want to endure more hair loss, body aches, and other unpleasant symptoms I was already experiencing.

In September of 2015, after six months of walking and many dietary changes, I decided to start thyroid medication. I was overcome with exhaustion and needed to do something different.

In the coming months, my lab tests revealed that my cholesterol and blood sugar were above normal limits. I was frustrated and made an appointment with the endocrinologist. Her explanation was that I needed to keep track of what I ate and write it down.

She said, "Those who have been through what you have can become depressed. Are you depressed? If so, I can give you something for that."

What? It was frustration; that was what I was feeling. I had to admit that at this point, my frustration turned to anger. I cried and screamed in the car on the way home from Seattle. After that, I decided to eat whatever I wanted, with smaller portions. Healthy drinks, fresh fruit, and veggies (which I'd been doing for months now) and just relax and take some pressure off myself. This struggle was not up to me, and the outcome was going to be achieved through my strength and faith. What else do I have to go through? What is my purpose? I continued to walk weekly and was adamant about moving forward.

Two months later, in January 2016, I went skiing for the day. My mind wanted to will my body to move faster. I'd been walking three miles a day for ten months now, but still my energy was just not there. Winded and frustrated, I kept going and knew that the more I progressed, the more Glenn would feel that I was on the recovery train. I certainly could not ski like before cancer. He maintained his love, support, and encouragement.

It took me two days to recover in bed. On the third day, we went for a seven-mile bike ride on a local trail (I didn't know at the time I'd gone that far). We stopped for rest and water and then continued on. His encouragement was instrumental for me. He would say that I was not a very patient person. This was true, and after all of my perceived hard work, I expected results. It would be a long, long process before results came. I'd really given up on the daily pressure on myself. With limited energy, I had to focus only on what I perceived to be most important: a healthy lifestyle and exercise.

Now seven months after starting thyroid medication, I am beginning to feel some much-needed energy return. Last month, a week vacation and three days of skiing gave me the jump-start once again to better health. Every day, I start new, and I know it's going to be a day-to-day process of determination to stay active and healthy. It's been what I feel is a long eleven months. I am so incredibly grateful that I am alive and have been given a second chance.

There have been so many wonderful people who have been on this journey with me, lifting me up, and I thank you from the bottom of my heart. When folks ask me what they can do and how they can help someone who is dealing with a life-changing diagnosis and treatment, I tell them it doesn't take much to show someone you care. Don't hold back, listen to your heart, and that person will be forever grateful.

Today, I am surprised and happy to put on a skort (shorts with a skirt on top). I bought it last summer and could barely button it. It is now loose and comfortable. Only a slight difference in weight, but I feel stronger than ever and will accept physically what is. Like cancer, this does not define who I am! With love and gratitude, Jody

By the way, I'm humbled when I look around my home and see all of the love bestowed upon me and my family with gifts, cards, and memories of those who opened their big hearts and gave of themselves. That was you. ♥

CHAPTER 30

Reflection

Today, as I am directed by the Holy Spirit to write down my feelings after going through cancer treatment and all that it encompasses, everything else seems such small scale. As I sit and wait for the results of my MRI for my right knee, I am reflecting on things this morning. On Friday, which was six days ago, I was celebrating life and looking forward to skiing at Whistler, BC, for the first time in years. With new ski boots in hand, I headed for an indoor ski facility to try out my boots before leaving on vacation. Twenty minutes of skiing, and the boots were great! The next thing I knew, I'd lost my balance at the end of the carpet, doing the splits and falling over.

Fast forward to urgent care, six x-rays, and an orthopedist visit later brings us to today. A brace, crutches, and today's MRI. As you can probably imagine by now, skiing is out of the question. For days, I have prayed that no permanent damage was done. As I lay on the MRI table, looking up at the cloud-enhanced lights (which are lovely, by the way), with my eyes closed, I continue to ask God for healing. I was at a loss for words, as I had asked for so many things in the past week. As the music started in my headset to distract me from the loud noise of the machine, this song came on: "Say What You Need to Say." It put me into silence as to not hear anything else around me. Was this a prompt by Him? I'm always in awe of the ways God can be heard. I do feel that I'm really listening a lot for His direction and grace on a daily basis.

As I wait, I realize that I had another surgery scheduled for a bilateral breast revision. This means that the implant on the left will be taken out and replaced by a smaller one. This is the one that was put in after the mastectomy and to this day continues to give me pain and cause back spasms. I had my preoperative appointment last week, and it was then two weeks until surgery. However, due to the knee injury, I found out today that this surgery cannot move forward. I feel very disappointed, but I know that God must have another plan for me.

A friend came over yesterday and asked what I was going to do while the rest of my family was skiing. I did not have a plan, since I was hoping to be skiing too. She suggested I take my laptop and write this book, since I had time. Was that what God wanted from me now? I do feel some urgency in getting to a point of having it edited. My goal was to finish the manuscript before surgery. I guess with that off the table, I'm free to finish. I pray for healing and strength together with the direction in which my days should be spent. On the other hand, I feel sad that after everything in the past five years, I am still not able to ski and spend the day with my loving husband and family in the beautiful wilderness of British Columbia.

Fast forward to December 29, 2016. It turns out that I fractured my lateral tibia on my right knee. It was so small that it was difficult to even see on the MRI. With eight weeks of crutches and no walking on the right leg, I went to Whistler, rented a wheelchair, and spent the days working on my manuscript. It was frustrating, looking out the snow-covered windows and not being able to ski with the family. I returned home after a week to start physical therapy. This was more painful than expected. I told myself that I would do exactly what the doctor told me to, whether I liked it or not (more on the "not" side).

Three miles a day was not only out of the question, it was impossible! I rented a lightweight wheelchair. This was fun. However, it proved to be more energy-consuming than I had imagined. I used it three times. I really enjoyed getting outside and breathing the fresh air. Sitting inside and not using my leg was starting to wear on my attitude. Thankfully, I was tired and in a fair amount of discomfort after physical therapy, so I didn't have the gumption most days to get out and about.

I did manage to do some light grocery shopping in a motorized wheelchair. You really find out a lot when you're put into a position of needing assistance. So many incredibly nice people are willing to help. I discovered many products at eye level, being in a wheelchair. I just realized that it was only temporary for me. One time, I was sitting in my car and just thought, *Ugh, no, I cannot go in today. I just don't have the energy.*

On another trip, I called a friend ahead of time to see if she could meet me at my house to carry my groceries inside. When I was done shopping, I asked if I could get assistance in getting the groceries into the car. A nice young boy unloaded them into my car. I wanted to give him a gift card as a thank you, but he declined. I was disappointed. He said that next time I saw someone in need that I should pass on the help to that person. What a nice kid. I was humbled right there.

The next trip to shop was during the holidays. When I arrived, there were no electric carts except one in which a man sitting. He had an oxygen tank and was waiting for his wife. He offered me his cart with such grace. I guess he saw me sitting on the bench, contemplating my next move with my crutches. There are such good people in the world. This always renews my spirit. Nobody really wants to have to depend on anyone else for help, even if they need it. I've been saying, "Thank you," a lot in the past two months. Feels so good.

On December 20, 2016, only eight weeks after my injury, I saw the orthopedic surgeon. They took x-rays, and the word was the fracture was healed! My prayers were answered. This downtime has given me the opportunity to finish what I started, however emotionally draining the process has been. There were days that I did not want to continue. By the grace of God and trust that He has a plan, I remain.

While I have another ten-week recovery ahead, combined with physical therapy, I'm excited to once again move forward. Starting to walk again has been so wonderful. There have been a few challenges. Hip soreness and weakness on the right side have kept me close to home. I do pray that my body will be restored and without pain after this recovery. My goal is to be able to ski on our next trip, which is planned for February.

CONCLUSION

Last evening, as I pondered a title for this book, it came to me: *It's Not about Me.* Let me back up a minute. Over the past several days, I have asked for guidance in prayer, since Glenn was looking for a men's group or a personal growth class or just something to further his journey. You get the idea. I decided to look up the above title to see if it was already being used. In fact, it is. An author by the name of Max Lucado has a book with that title. I brushed it off and didn't give it another thought.

As I said my prayers before bed, something guided me to take a second look at Lucado's book to find out what it's about. As the book loads on my phone, I realize it's not about me at all. It's about you: the you, as in my spouse. It turns out that *It's Not about Me* is a book on spiritual journey. It has a workbook to accompany it. I was so excited to share this news with Glenn. Here I thought I was listening for a title to my own book, but instead, I was being led to discover the answer to my prayer, God is good.

Final update, sent 7/8/17 10:08 a.m.
Subject: Closure for This Season

From May 2011, when I was diagnosed with breast cancer, to today, six years have passed. I've learned so much about many things: health and nutrition, myself, and most of all, people in general. My life has changed tremendously during this time. I remember Dr. Rinn saying to continue to move, even if it is just a walk to the end of the street. This was so instrumental in my physical and emotional wellness. There were days when this short walk was all I had in me. There were days I didn't even have this in me. I had a support system of so many people in my community; my friends and neighbors volunteered to walk with me. Most of the time, I chose to walk with Glenn. It was a time where emotions welled, and walking, sometimes in silence, was therapeutic. Our family managed to still get away on many occasions for some time together, which I believe helped keep things as close to normal as possible. One of my closest friends accompanied us on many trips. She spent time with me and allowed Glenn to spend time with the kids without being concerned about me. She is a gift, and I am forever grateful to have such a beautiful person in my life. After my treatments were finished, she and I began walking every day those three miles during her lunch hour from work. She doesn't know that many of those days, I didn't feel like walking. I came home every day and had to rest for several hours after walking. It took everything I had and a very long time to regain my energy. She doesn't know just how important she was in keeping me accountable. It can be challenging getting past your own emotional upset, but it really kept me focused on the world around me rather than succumbing to my own feelings.

I received many books that would nurture my soul and give me hope. Here are a few of them:

- *Daily Journey of HOPE*, Family Christian Stores
- *Stronger than Cancer Book,* by Connie Payton
- *20 Ways to Make Every Day Better,* by Joyce Meyer

With this particular season of my life coming to a close, I am looking ahead to many more adventures and remaining well. While I am a cancer survivor, there are still the years of continual monitoring and tests. I have to take a hormone blocker (Letrozole). It keeps my body from producing estrogen, which feeds the cancer cells. It is taken for ten years after treatment. Now, every six months, I see my oncologist and go to the lab to have my blood drawn. It's different now since the port on my chest has been removed. The scar is still there. Wounds from battle. They don't bother me as much anymore. They are just a reminder of a time from the past.

I sometimes cannot believe how much I've gone through. My faith has carried me around every corner, not knowing how I would get through the next surgery or MRI. I take one day at a time and am thankful. I believe we each have a purpose. I have a second chance to live and to love.

I have much to reflect upon. During the last few years, I have completely changed the way I eat. I have found that the food I eat not only nourishes the body and can heal from the inside but can prevent further detriment down the road. Here are a few reference books I learned a great deal from:

- *Nature's Prescription for Optimum Health, Nutribullet Rx Book*
- Nutribullet Natural Healing Foods
- *The Starch Solution*, by John A. McDougall
- *Plant Strong*, by Rip Esselstyn

As we prepare to send the last of our three kids off to college, I realize that so much has happened during this season. I have a lot of feelings: happiness, sadness, gratitude, and mostly, so thankful that I am still here. Only time will reveal what is to come next.

I've included photos from some of those times during the past six years and a current photo. I have exercised most of my life, so that's not new. Walking three miles a day for a couple of years has prepared me for biking seven miles a day. I can go farther on a bike. I have been cleared to ski moderately as I increase my strength after the small knee fracture. I skied several days last winter. I spent seven months in physical therapy during this time. Shelly, my physical therapist, has been my champion and prepared me each time for the next ski adventure. I was so excited to receive a special shirt after completing therapy. It says "Sore today, Stronger tomorrow." So true! I could not have done it without her. My goal is to get back to Whistler and ski again.

I've had several setbacks, but each one has propelled me further and made me stronger, not just physically but spiritually and emotionally. I do believe that there is a reason for each setback and that learning to overcome these obstacles propelled me forward. I have been knocked down many more times than I can mention and keep pressing on to become stronger for the next.

There is so much potential within us that I believe has not been tapped into until such a time presents itself. I am much stronger than I ever thought I was.

My spirit has been renewed, and as I further my walk, I find many things I have been led to that have helped strengthen me as an individual. We are all the same. It's what we do with our gifts and how we love others that can change how we view ourselves and the world. By lifting up others, we in turn are lifted up. As we reach out and touch lives, we lead by example: a compliment, a smile, a touch on the arm.

Recently, I encountered an ear, nose, and throat doctor. I was struck by the way he interacted with me as a patient. He explained things simply and while speaking, he genuinely touched my shoulder to indicate that he cared and was interested in my responses. Such a simple gesture, and yet so profound. There are small ways we can care for others, just by listening and acknowledging their feelings. My hope is that my journey will inspire and encourage you during your trials and, more importantly, give you hope. All the best.

CPSIA information can be obtained
at www.ICGtesting.com
Printed in the USA
LVHW01s2303130918
590134LV00001B/2/P

9 781973 633174